How to Value a Skylark

The Countryside in a Time of Change

Brian Kerr

How to Value a Skylark

The Countryside in a Time of Change

Brian Kerr

EVENTISPRESS

Published in Great Britain in 2020

By Eventispress

The cover illustration is *The Skylark* by Pam Grimmond.

A catalogue record for this book is available from the British Library.

ISBN 978-1-8381526-1-1

Printed by Ingram Sparks

To my children and grandchildren;

that they will find a countryside as full of beauty and

interest as I have.

I live my best in the landscape, being at ease there;

the only trouble I find I have brought in my hand.

See, I let it fall with a rustle of stems in the nettles,

and never for a moment suppose that they understand.

John Hewitt from 'The Ram's Horn'

from *John Hewlitt: Selected Poems*, eds.

Michael Longley and Frank Ormsby

(Blackstaff Press, 2007)

Reproduced by permission of Blackstaff Press

on behalf of The Estate of John Hewlitt.

LIST OF ILLUSTRATIONS

Pam Grimmond, a Yorkshire based artist and printmaker based at Markington, supplied the cover image of a skylark.

Richard Revels is a professional photographer based in Bedfordshire. His images are from within this county and appear on the rear cover and through the text. Many have already been published in the book, *Bedfordshire-our changing habitats and wildlife: A PHOTOGRAPHIC RECORD,* by Richard Revels, Graham Bellamy and Chris Boon, published by the Bedfordshire Natural History Society in 2020.

Joe Morris provided the picture of flooded land in Chapter 5.

Vaughan Dean provided the images of Somerset at the beginning of the book and the view of the power station from Ampthill Great Park in Chapter 6.

Aileen Irvine supplied the images of the Mourne Mountains, Co Down, Northern Ireland also used in Chapter 6.

Andy Knight provided the image of Ampthill Great Park in Chapter 9.

Lisa King supplied the view of Shuttleworth College in Chapter 10.

Jim Trolinger is acknowledged for use of his painting of Flitwick Woods which follows Chapter 11.

All other images are by the author **Brian Kerr**.

Frontispiece illustration:

Sharpenhoe Clappers, Bedfordshire

This prominent Bedfordshire landmark, close to the village of Barton-le Clay, is crowned by beech woodland, and is a designated Site of Special Scientific Interest and also within the Chilterns, Area of Outstanding Natural Beauty (AOSB). The site is a fragment of a cultural landscape, and is of interest as a historic monument, with an Iron Age promontory fort, and evidence of use as a managed rabbit warren in the 15th century. The beech tree cover is typical of the shallow soils on the chalk escarpment. The area is managed by the National Trust and is a popular walking area giving access to a neighbouring Country Park, and the ancient Icknield Way route, crossing eastern England. (Photograph by Richard Revels)

Back cover illustrations:

Skylark in Flight

The skylark is notoriously difficult to photograph, nesting in dense cover on the ground and often identified only by vibrant song. Disturbance by dogs and walkers in the critical spring nesting season is now a real threat to skylark numbers. (Photograph by Richard Revels)

Brown Hares boxing in spring

The countryside of eastern England with large fields is now a prime location for illegal hare coursing. Farmers are often threatened, and policing over large areas is difficult. There is concern that this activity is increasing. Shooting of hares for sport has no close season in England and Wales, unlike in Scotland. (Photograph by Richard Revels)

CONTENTS

PREFACE

This book begins with skylarks. In the spring of 2018, four skylarks climbed above the rough grass field, their fast, rich, song drawing us into our garden to try to spot the birds high against the blue sky. In his book, *Our Place: Can we save Britain's Wildlife before it is too late?* Mark Cocker describes these spring calls as, *'the fresh sunlight rain-showered skylarks' song'*.[1] The birdsong was replaced the following spring with the brain-pounding thump of a pile-driver banging supports into the field as foundations for new housing. The birds had gone. This was hardly a surprise: the field on the edge of a small popular Bedfordshire town had long been a target for development and now the informal rough grass and the handy short-cut to the local school had disappeared. By the end of the decade there was a neat housing estate.

Why did this make an impact? After all, the statistics were clear: in Britain, there had been roughly a 75 per cent decline in skylarks from the 1970s to the millennium.[2] Perhaps this small, very local loss of a few birds had made the changes around us real. The numbers of all farmland birds were in decline. We had read the reports, but these were *our* skylarks that welcomed each springtime, and so it was directly relevant. Set against the rising alarm around global warming, the loss of the Amazon rainforest, forest fires, melting glaciers, intense storms and the decline in wildlife across the countryside, the loss of a few birds in one field in southern England was a mere trifle. However, there was a personal message: the landscape and wildlife were changing fast. The trends seemed remorseless and the pace increasing.

In 2014, I was encouraged to publish a non-technical book, which provided an outline of the making of the landscape in one English county, Bedfordshire. This was followed, in 2019, by a second publication which traced chronologically the impact of people in this typical part of lowland southern England.[4] During the decade from 2010, local newspapers have been full of accounts of planned 'garden cities' and an arc of housing across a swathe of southern England, to link Oxford to Cambridge and deliver a million homes. The high-speed rail (HS2) to the north of England is expected to rip through five protected nature reserves: 33 Sites of Special Scientific Interest (SSSIs); 693 classified local nature reserves; and 108 ancient woodlands.[3] Nature is in trouble!

Ideally, this book would be a dispassionate account of the issues facing the British countryside and landscape at the beginning of 2020, which are likely to persist for a decade and beyond. This is not the case for a number of reasons. Firstly, every writer brings to the page a number of biases, which are difficult to overcome. My background in soil science has brought me into contact with farmers, foresters, environmentalists, engineers, economists and a few politicians. Although I have listened carefully and, I hope, politely to the passionate arguments, my only conclusion has been that reaching a consensus is difficult. What became clear in working on this book is that striving to reach a balance or agreement is where we are in Britain at present. There will be trade-offs required and the outcome will not satisfy all. Nevertheless, I have attempted to stick to the intention of presenting the arguments without overtly taking a position.

Secondly, throughout these chapters I have tried to underline the point that land and its use is an emotive topic. During the Covid-19 pandemic lockdown period of spring 2020, this was made very explicit. There were complaints about trespassing, fly-tipping and fires on moorland. The disparity between those with access to greenspace and those with little opportunity to enjoy the outdoors was laid bare. The impacts on health and well-being became a political issue.

The subtitle of this book – *The Countryside in a Time of Change* – points out that we live in a period of upheaval, and the pandemic emergency has only added to the many questions we will have to face during the coming decade. There are often strident voices. This Preface was written in July 2020, following a headline in the morning paper: *'People want to create a greener happier world. But our politicians have other ideas'.*[5] These divides are real, pitting developers against conservationists and those wanting greater access against land managers. Finding common ground – literally – was always a challenge.

The aspiration has been to map and provide a brief background to some of these issues, with an emphasis on how the future looks for the countryside and landscapes across Britain. The primary aim is to make this account both non-technical and accessible. Statistics are sprinkled throughout the text and are used to press home the arguments, but this is kept to a minimum. Although this new book uses examples and includes illustrations from Bedfordshire to back up the text, the nature of the issues outlined here reaches well beyond one county and these arguments resonate across Britain. Since agriculture is a devolved government responsibility, care has been taken to specify if figures refer to England and Wales, to all of Britain or, more rarely, across all the UK. Where possible, sources for facts and figures are provided as endnotes at the back of the book. There is also a list of further reading materials, which includes useful books for those interested in exploring more of the background on specific topics. This book was written in a hurry. The issues are changing fast and therefore errors are likely. However, the main thrust should be clear.

Finally, this book was begun before the word 'Covid-19' meant anything and writing continued during lockdown. There has been much speculation around the potentially lasting impacts which the dramatic events of early 2020 may have on the countryside and our attitude towards the environment. For example, will the renewed interest in the outdoors, which led to an upsurge in walking and cycling, be maintained, or will there be a return to the previous level of car use? Will the funding of new cycle routes still be welcomed when these lead to disrupted traffic flows?

The final chapter is a postscript to summarize a few of these speculative thoughts. What is clear is that the issues outlined in this book are not about to disappear. The glorious weather across Britain in spring 2020, which made lockdown more bearable, was also the driest on record, bringing into focus long-term climatic trends and a corresponding and significant reduction in harvest yields.

One positive aspect of the lockdown was that friends and colleagues, freed from their daily routine, were open to reading and commenting on the text. A feature of this period was the surge in reporting on the countryside and wildlife. The challenge in writing was to keep abreast of the tide. I am most grateful to everyone who supplied ideas and corrected my misunderstandings.

I acknowledge the valuable help of Maurice and Carolyn Gowdy, Colin Calvert, Ian Baillie and Jon Balaam for their patience in correcting the early drafts and, at the same time, pointing out emerging news stories.

Gale Winskill supplied a professional edit and, as with previous publications, Diana Jackson from Eventispress undertook the layout and nursed the book through the publication process. Without professional advice and encouragement from both, this text would never have progressed beyond a few random ideas.

I am pleased to acknowledge the permission given to use the skylark artwork by Pam Grimmond on the book cover. Within the text, I am especially grateful to Richard Revels for the use of professional images from his extensive collection of wildlife and the countryside. Aileen Irvine permitted the use of her photographs of the Mourne Mountains in County Down and also guided me and others on a memorable walk into those hills. Vaughan Dean kindly supplied images of various parts of England. All other images are my own. Throughout the writing, my wife Elizabeth has provided both practical assistance and, more importantly, encouragement.

To all these people and others unnamed, I am very grateful. This Preface began with the skylark, an iconic bird of the British countryside. It has not been difficult to find verses celebrating skylarks to include in the opening pages. During the period of most severe lockdown many people rediscovered birdsong, including that of skylarks, during country walks, leading to a recognition of what is being lost from the landscape.

In the spring of 2019, I led a walk on the Dunstable Downs above Luton. The wheat crops were a healthy green, the sky blue and the paths cut into the clear white chalk. Looking back at a field of early wheat I was puzzled by the frequency of neat geometric squares in the growing crop. A fellow walker explained that these were left after the field was drilled in the autumn. Skylarks used these patches convenient as nest sites and this added to the nesting opportunities, along with the broad headlands, at the field margin on which we walked. The hope is that farmland birds will be encouraged to nest here and their decline will be slowed as a result.

Will this and other small conservation changes have the desired outcome? Will the response be adequate? Is this what the balance of interest requires? What do we expect from the countryside and how much value can be placed on individual habitats?

These are the questions at the heart of this book.

Ampthill, September, 2020

A Green Imagined Land

This view of Lussombe, Somerset is often what is perceived as the typical countryside of England, made up from essential elements such as a prominent church tower and small hamlet, framed by green fields, and bounded by neat hedgerows. Closer inspection can often reveal clues to the history of the landscape. The well-tended hedge with a fence in the foreground is in contrast to the hedge in the middle picture which has residual larger trees: the patch of scrubland behind the church may have been cultivated and reverted to scrub. This is now backed by ranks of planted conifers, in contrast to the older mixed woods in the background. This area is within the Exmoor National Park. (Photograph by Vaughan Dean)

INTRODUCTION

Public Funds and Public Goods

As Britain approached the end of 2019, there was an unmistakable sense that things were about to change, and quickly. 'Business as usual' was no longer an option. Elections brought a new Government and the UK's departure from the European Union became a reality. Extinction Rebellion demonstrators were on the streets and the background flow of media coverage of global climatic change became difficult to ignore. Australian bush fires claimed lives, destroyed homes and wiped out an estimated half a billion animals.[1] Despite the graphic pictures of dead and injured animals, the numbers were difficult to absorb, but the message was the same: the global climate was changing and there would be big challenges locally, nationally and globally. Climate events would have a real, direct and local impact on how we live.

In early 2020, severe flooding swamped homes and businesses across large areas of Britain. There was an acceptance that new ideas were needed, which complemented the building of more and higher flood defences. Holding water on the land before the flood surge reached the already swollen rivers was at least part of the answer. These events and their potential solutions brought land and how we use it back into the national debate. This book is one response to those questions, and tries to understand how these changes may play out across the British countryside.

The language used to convey these messages was altering too. In a few months we had gone from 'global warming' to a 'climate emergency'. The countryside was now required to provide 'ecosystem services' and we were asked to evaluate the land and wildlife habitats using new measures referred to as 'Natural Capital Accounting'.

At end of January 2020, the Government added a suite of new policy ideas on the environment, land and how to fund agriculture in England. Farmers were perplexed and concerned over the prospect of cheaper food imports and the payment of subsidies. Those interested in conservation and the environment were increasingly worried by the noise over any potential move away from European standards on food and conservation, and how any new funding arrangements post-Brexit would operate.

A radical new policy on the land was signalled in the January, 2020 Agriculture Bill, at the heart of which was public funding through tax for what were described as 'public goods', meaning a swing away from the previous drive to maximize food production. Would this new priority on the environment really mean more access to the countryside, new nature areas, the return of hedgerows and the conservation of ancient woodlands?[2] The 2019 election campaign threw up a surprising interest in tree-planting, with the parties bidding to reach levels in the millions, ignoring fundamental questions on: the land to be used; the types of tree species planted; where tree saplings would come from; how these woods would be looked after; and the ongoing depletion of existing ancient woodlands.

Throughout this fog of anxiety there was also some excitement and the welcoming of new and radical ideas arguing that the existing national approach of confining nature to reserves, fenced off from commercial agriculture, was no longer feasible. A more innovative idea was to step back and let nature take over. In some areas where this had been tried, the results were exciting. 'Rewilding' became a discussion point and there was intense interest in small-scale experiments in several parts of England. Suddenly lynx in Northumberland and beavers in Somerset became more likely.

The message was clear: change across the countryside was underway and happening fast. Could it really be the 'managed transition' described by politicians, or the more alarming prospect of higher temperatures and increased flooding driving change as described by scientists? It was becoming difficult to separate one issue from another. A blizzard of new words and terminology made it difficult to discern the real concerns. Could potential opportunities emerge as changes took place?

Other trends were also pushing for attention, such as the marked change in food preferences, bringing plant-based diets into the mainstream and leading to a reduced role for livestock production and the dairy industry across Britain. The race to replace fossil fuels boosted the renewable-energy sector, prompting the questions: How many on-shore wind farms are desirable? And can land be usefully shared with photovoltaic solar panels? Each initiative has a potential impact on land and how it is used across a small island. The difficulty is then in separating out the priorities and thinking through responses.

Then came a pandemic emergency and a national lockdown. One outcome was the discovery – or rediscovery – of the importance of being outdoors and in contact with nature. This underlined forcibly the importance of access to the countryside and its impact on physical and mental health. Nature became the 'go-to' place for many in a time of confusion and anxiety. With the Covid-19 pandemic, the role of parks and countryside as a significant factor in health and well-being was given greater recognition. The job description of the countryside and land managers was growing longer all the time. This prompted consideration of: What do we expect from the countryside? How do we decide priorities and make value judgements?

One way to approach this problem, unlikely as it seems, is to think like Donald Rumsfeld! The US Secretary of State, in a speech in February 2002 concerning the Iraq War and its impacts, offered a handy analysis tool. Rumsfeld divided the future into, 'known unknowns' and 'unknown unknowns'. Behind this seemingly tortured syntax is a real truth. There is a consensus that climate change will affect the way in which agriculture operates. but we have only a very sketchy understanding of how this will play out, especially across global food production – this is a *known unknown*; we accept this is happening, but the details remain an unknown.[3]

The real danger lies in the impacts of *unknown unknowns*; for instance, a sudden change in the political balance, a slowing of international trade, a breakdown in international security, an increase in cyber-attacks, or a new pandemic such as coronavirus. All are unknowns and therefore impossible or difficult to prepare for.

Changes will almost certainly make an impact on many aspects of life in Britain, including the countryside as we perceive it.

Numerous writers have charted the pathway of evolution and change across the landscapes of Britain, and all have made the fundamental point that countryside and landscape are anything but static. The landscape history of England is lovingly described by WG Hoskins, in *The Making of the English Landscape,* which provides a readable and perceptive insight into what we see in the countryside today.[4] RN Millman complemented this with a similar account for Scotland.[5] Therefore, the changes presently on the horizon are only the latest in the evolving relationship we have with nature, the countryside and what we would like to see outdoors. These alterations have been profound in the past, with the pattern of the modern landscape in lowland England being set with regular fields and hedges, which transformed the land following enclosures from 1750 onwards.

More recently, the diversification of the countryside, in response to the demands of the leisure industry and a decline in farm incomes, has changed its appearance once more. A field of grazing llamas is no longer unusual. Even the recent campaigns to plant millions of trees is an echo of an earlier panic referred to as 'oak mania', when in the seventeenth century, there was alarm over the supply of timber for the navy. Naval officers were urged to carry acorns and plant these in English estates when on shore leave!

Early chapters in this book explore the major factors which influence what we presently see in the land and how these may change, beginning with agriculture. Farming will undoubtedly be impacted by how farm businesses are funded and the emphasis we place on food production and the security of supply. How much land do we need to secure food supply and how intensively do we want farming to be? Also, how much tree cover is needed, and how many trees can realistically be planted? Alternatively, how much land can be dedicated to woodland in an effort to reduce global warming? These are political questions that hinge on the national approach to climate change and the target of a carbon-neutral economy in Britain by 2050.

Into this needs to be woven the urgent need to halt the decline of biodiversity across the countryside and the effort to restore functioning habitats which can act as buffers against changing climate. All of these major issues are interconnected and thinking in separate compartments will mean limit effectiveness. The response to increased levels of flooding throughout both England and Scotland has illustrated that thinking, which is constrained by focusing on one solution; different ideas on how we use land overall are required.

If we then place land and its use at the centre, any rethinking about the countryside quickly bumps up against the market cost of acquiring any patch of land. With land prices steadily increasing, the scope to influence change is constrained. History has shown there are few more politically sensitive topics as land – who owns it and how it is used.

The ability of the land to meet often-competing pressures is now being tested using economic approaches which have begun to inject values, costs and prices into the thinking. This will always be controversial. The base assumption is we can place a value on one aspect of nature or on a habitat and measure the costs and benefits of the services provided by, for example, a wood or a meadow. This goes against the grain for many and underlines the ethical, as well as the practical, arguments that underpin technical economics.

Nevertheless, many of the required and planned proposals and changes will need generous funding from 'public funds' to achieve so-called 'public goods'. These choices depend on sorting out priorities and then assigning perhaps arbitrary or estimated values. The changes are gathering speed and ranking importance is difficult and necessitates major trade-offs, which will ultimately be debated in public. Past controversies on policy choices, such as the route of HS2 or the future of grouse moors, are likely to be typical of what to expect before a trade-off is reached. In the context of very tight budget forecasts for the coming decade, arriving at the 'value' of any 'service' provided by a habitat or single farm could generate a heated argument.

Understanding these arguments may not demand a detailed knowledge of economics. However, some understanding of the language and background of the issues, may contribute to this debate.

A grasp of the likely outcomes in terms of the 'public goods' and benefits delivered is best arrived at by some knowledge of what is in the 'public interest.'

This is where the value of skylarks and their place in the countryside may become something we hear more of.

Public footpaths as public good

The extensive network of paths across the countryside in England and Wales is an example of what economists call a 'public good'. These are open to all without cost and are well used by many. The paths do need maintenance however, and without voluntary efforts by ramblers groups there is a danger that this public asset will diminish. The substantial increase in their use in 2020 illustrates the importance of a well maintained path, providing access to the countryside for all.

A public good: a bit like a lighthouse

This book covers a range of topics which are, increasingly, receiving media attention and likely to gather momentum over the next ten years. Many of these issues are contested and the language used can be difficult to penetrate. Familiar words surface in unfamiliar combinations and have a specific meaning, such as the increasingly used term, 'the public good', which is borrowed from economics. Behind the radical changes proposed for British agriculture, there is frequent reference to 'public goods for public funds' — that is, for taxpayers' money.

Public goods are, as the name implies, simply goods and services which are available to all and of benefit to all. In addition, no individual can be excluded: their use by one person does not reduce the overall benefit to others. This is a 'good' or 'service', which can be used simultaneously by many. Examples abound, such as street lighting, clean air, or a flood-protection scheme.

The example often used to illustrate the idea of a 'public good' is a lighthouse: available to all seafarers at no cost to shipping, and visible to many boats at one time — it is not exclusive.

CHAPTER ONE

A New Furrow[1]

In the first quarter of the nineteenth century the Board of Agriculture sent inspectors on horseback throughout England, with instructions to produce an account of the nation's farming. The idea was to bring together a general picture of agriculture following the enclosure of the large landed estates in the late eighteenth and early nineteenth centuries. A rapidly growing urban population which needed to be fed, as well as mounting concerns over security and strife in mainland Europe, all added to the political concern. There was danger that social unrest would spread and a prudent government was looking at national food security. Although the intention was to improve agriculture overall, the main emphasis was on the arable counties, with the production of grain for bread-making an immediate worry. Bedfordshire, for example, was surveyed in 1808, and again in 1813, and the records show the county was then noted for the growing of barley and some market gardening.[2]

Food security in Britain has remained a political issue and has surfaced at regular intervals throughout recent history. There was a flurry of interest in the media in the run-up to the departure from the European Union (EU) and disruption at the beginning of the 2020 global pandemic again brought a focus on the fragility of our food supply.[3] As the media agonized over flour and pasta, the public was busy buying seeds and preparing to grow fresh produce. Seed companies were forced to close their websites in April 2020 as demand mounted. There remains public anxiety over extended food-supply chains. In wartime, the remedy was rationing and a ploughing-up campaign: in peacetime, the prospect of empty supermarket shelves always causes alarm. 'Backing British farming in a volatile world' is a frequent plea from the agricultural lobby.

This is the historical background to any future changes in the pattern of farming across Britain and is the context for the promised agricultural reforms required by the UK's departure from the EU. A few statistics are required to grapple with this potential shake-up. The present balance of home-grown food in the UK is usually accepted as around half of consumption. During the Brexit debate these figures were challenged by the argument that food processed in the UK is often taken as 'home-produced', whereas the raw ingredients are imported. The balance then becomes as high as a 75-per-cent dependency on imports.[4] The level of imports contributes to the debate over food miles, fair trade, animal welfare and other global sustainability issues.

There is agreement that the direction of travel since the war has been towards more food imports, which have risen steadily, as any supermarket fruit and vegetable aisle will show. However, the old spectre of food security has not entirely gone away and access to future food supplies lies in the dimly lit world of tariffs, trade deals and common standards. Additionally, future deals to ensure the uninterrupted flow of food will be set against the overall importance of agriculture to the UK economy.

Previously, subsidies to British farmers from the EU were worth around £3.1 billion per year, and there are many pledges that this level of support will continue, at least until the end of 2021. Farm support will then embark on a transition, which will replace the direct subsidy – the Basis Scheme Payment (BSP) –calculated presently on the farmed area. New payment arrangements will be targeted specifically towards the delivery of what are now called 'public goods'. The aspiration is that such measures will help sustain a rural economy, reverse, or at least halt, the decline in biodiversity and play a part in the UK's efforts to counter climate change by contributing to a carbon-neutral budget by 2050. The outlines of these reforms are set out in the Agriculture Bill introduced in January 2020. At the centre of this new policy is the determination to invest in overall environmental enhancement, with significant gains in carbon storage and a marked reduction in greenhouse-gas emissions.[5]

The headline to take from these Government proposals is the move towards 'public goods' for the spending of 'public funds'. In other words, the farming sector will be at the forefront of the promised environmental changes. This is a fundamental swing away from food production as the clear and single priority, which has dominated agriculture across the UK since the Second World War. The aspirations explained in the legislation include a gain in environmental benefits, which include flood protection, the storing of carbon, conservation of wildlife, maintenance of healthy soils and access to the countryside. These are now regarded as important aspects of farming and rank as positive benefits, alongside the traditional job of producing food for the plate. However, if the pledges move the agricultural sector towards priorities other than food production and elevate environmental concerns to a higher level of priority, then there will be a corresponding need to place greater emphasis on the commercial farming sector. Only in this way can the UK ensure a level of home-grown food production, which is acceptable to consumers.

Commercial crops and a tidy countryside

Oil seed rape in now an established part of the arable cropping system usually as a 'break' crop in a rotation with wheat. These fields near Toddington in Bedfordshire are typical of much of arable lowland Britain in the spring. (Photograph by Richard Revels).

CAP is dead: long live ELMS

During the Brexit debate the design of the EU system of farm payments, known as the Common Agricultural Policy (CAP), was frequently cited as needing radical reform. Papers from the UK Department of Agriculture and Rural Affairs (Defra), described the CAP as 'deeply flawed' and many environmentalists, and indeed some farmers, would agree. Breaking with the CAP, it was argued, could only be achieved by a national scheme tailored to the needs of British farmers. A main objection to this CAP framework was the principle of area payments which, at the basic level, were paid to active farmers based solely on the amount of farmed land. There was no cap on the amounts paid, so bigger farm businesses accrued annual sums totalling around £3 million from the Basic Farm Subsidy alone. In simple terms: the bigger the farm, the more cash it accumulated.

In order to gain enhanced environmental benefits from the land, additional funds were offered at a higher level, which rewarded 'environmental stewardship', defined by such practices as looking after hedgerows, leaving wide headland strips at the edge of fields and planting trees. Given that almost three-quarter of the land in the UK is presently used for farming in some way or other, any future radical change to these payments has the potential to change the appearance of the countryside.

By flipping the payments in any future budget and making environmental and conservation a priority, the subsidy system becomes a very powerful lever for the Government to encourage a move towards environmental protection and enhancement. The reality is then that food production is no longer the overriding priority for British land.

In 2018, Michael Gove, the then Minister for the Environment, signalled this radical change for England and Wales in the proposed Agricultural Bill, (agriculture in Scotland and Northern Ireland is devolved to regional administrations, which may decide to support farms in different ways). The phrase used was 'rewarding public goods', and listed planting trees and hedges, restoring peatlands and taking steps to encourage nesting birds. All these were to be recognized and funded.

The new framework has been entitled the 'Environmental Land Management System' (ELMS), and the importance of the *environment* is in the title. Although some farmers are excited by being paid for acting as countryside stewards, there is a worry that smaller farms will not have the capacity to earn adequate rewards. Two-thirds of British farms have already ventured into complementary business ventures, ranging from bed and breakfast to farm shops, or on-farm cheese-making. Many enterprises make more money from these businesses than from farming.

The previous CAP system was based on an entirely different philosophy, taking into account the wide divergency across European farming systems. At the heart of this concept was income support to keep active farmers on the land. Farming was then the means to prevent a decline in the rural sector across Europe. As such, this was an economic solution to a political problem. ELMS, in contrast, is conditional on environmental improvements, paid by results. This means the money spent actually achieves an improvement in resource management. Additionally, these payments are not tied to 'active farming', so the funds need to be spread across uplands and non-farming areas, which may be a better investment in terms of environmental return. So, a grouse moor which reclaims peat moorland and can demonstrate an improved upland environment for wildlife may be a better bet for an ELMS payment than an arable lowland farm.

On the other hand, lowland farms close to centres of population may gain from schemes which award permissive public access to more land.. Footpaths illustrate the gap that remains until the new ELMS arrangement is in operation: many agreements on the use of permissive paths, agreed under European funding, have expired, or will do soon. A farmer then faces a choice: risk the opposition of a local community now familiar with this footpath, or hold on in the expectation of a new tranche of payments.

Therefore, the EU-funded CAP, denigrated as it was, provided an economic safety net for large parts of the agricultural industry, and there is considerable nervousness around overturning these payments. In England they represent around 60 per cent of farm income, rising to as much as 80 per cent in other parts of the UK. Without an underpinning subsidy, around 40 per cent of all farms will declare an annual loss. Paradoxically, in late 2019, the EU launched a radical overhaul of the CAP, which is to be replaced by the so-called *'Farm-to-Fork Strategy',* which is a part of the new European Green Deal, which will also take Europe along the same path of environmental support.[6]

During 2020, the Government embarked on a wide-ranging consultation exercise with the farming community. Early results from this indicate that there is a lack of trust with the previous Countryside Stewardship Scheme and this will need to be rebuilt to ensure wide acceptance of any new arrangement such as ELMS. As many of the payments will be based on characteristics which are difficult to measure with precision, there will need to be a willingness to change if there is a lack of farmer support. At the heart of this scheme is the acceptance that farmers are paid to achieve 'public goods'. Although there is agreement on the general principle, the exact definition of what is a *public benefit* is still unclear, and the measurements needed to trigger payments are yet to be defined. Then comes the challenge of selling these ideas to a sceptical farming audience.

Many conservation organizations such as Wildlife Trusts either own or manage land and therefore also warrant funding. Any fall in the basic payments presently available would certainly blow a hole in the tightly managed conservation budget. Therefore, the proposed ELMS subsidy payments have a large funding gap to plug. A policy update on how the transition will be managed, during the period to late 2024, illustrates the future difficulties which face farmers during this period of change.[7]

The intention is that by late 2024, the UK will be embarking in a new direction. There will be losers as well as winners in the countryside, and the public debate will be centred on core topics such as food security, keeping farmers who are willing to act as countryside stewards on their farms, and the willingness of the public to accept the principle of public funds being spent in return for public goods. Given that the payments are no longer coming from Brussels, this debate will be of concern to all UK taxpayers. How much do we really care about healthy soils or nesting skylarks? What do we most want from the countryside?

When it comes to issues around farming, the British public often turns to the BBC and *The Archers.* In the autumn of 2016, broadcasts featured a protracted row over how the soils at Brookfield Farm were being treated, with Adam advocating the brave new world of 'no-till' cropping and Brian not quite convinced. Exactly how commercial farmers look after their soil became a surprisingly passionate argument for a national programme, with Adam making the point strongly that present machinery uses expensive diesel and being heavy, *'knocked six bells out of the top soil, which is the magic layer full of microbes, organisms and worms.'*[8] The alternative was to simply scratch the surface and plant seed directly into stubble land. Included in the Government's new ELMS proposals is the promotion of a 'healthy soil' as a recommendation: defining a healthy soil may be difficult, but *The Archers* were ahead of the Government!

Suddenly soil was in the news, at least in *The Archers*. Dire warnings began to emerge that top soils in eastern England were especially vulnerable, and we needed to do more to protect this resource. Despite scientists urging caution on the gloomy forecasts, the subject was incorporated into the Government's proposals. This illustrates the difficulty faced when including this type of measurement into any new and workable subsidy framework. Under the former EU arrangements, the basic payments were simply based on size of the area farmed. How do you measure environmental benefits such as a healthy soil? How is this monitored after each crop, and at what level of payments? There is scope for substantial differences of opinions and as this involves money, the prospect of healthy rows.

A hundred harvests left: fake news or confused science?

Most gardeners will confidently tell you what an ideal soil is: dark in colour; never too wet, but holds moisture in a drought; deep enough for a trench to grow some potatoes; crumbles through the fingers; and of course, contains a few worms! Gardeners will then move quickly to complain about the soil in their patch: stony; or so wet in the winter that the harvesting of leeks is a muddy experience; or so dry in the summer that watering becomes a tedious business.

Farmers also will recognize a deep well-drained loam and are prepared to spend money on getting the nutrient balance right. The challenge, as always, is to squeeze a few more kilograms of wheat from the field. This attention to detail has been successful in that yields of wheat in England have increased steadily over the decade to 2017. The competition amongst growers led to attempts to crack the barrier of 10 tonnes per hectare required to be a member of the unofficial 'Ten-Tonne Club'. In 2015, a farm in Northumberland recorded over 16 tonnes from each hectare, and ambitious targets have been set to achieve 20 tonnes per hectare by 2030. Much of these yield gains have resulted from genetic improvements to the seed, but attention to soil preparation and fertility is critical. Farmers also worry about damage to the soil from increasingly heavy machinery; the loss of top soil, seed and fertilizer in the spring from wind-blow; and the more recent tendency for sudden heavy rain on unprotected soils, leading to rills and gullies in arable fields.

This begs the question: How far can we push finite soil resources to maintain or continually increase yields? In 2014, *Farmers Weekly* led with the headline, *'Only 100 harvests left in UK farm soils, scientists warn'*, quoting research from the University of Sheffield.[9] This concern was tapped into by the then Minister for the Environment, Michael Gove, who warned in a speech in 2017 that the UK was 30–40 years away from the 'eradication of soil fertility'.[10] The problem was that these scare headlines were repeated so frequently that they began to be accepted as a fact, which was difficult to counter. The claim of limited harvests cropped up again in 2020, in a BBC statistics programme, which questioned to what extent such headlines reflect the science.[11]

James Wong, writing in *The New Scientist* in early 2019, was also very sceptical.[12] A close reading of the research showed that there is widespread unease over the interpretation of the Sheffield findings, which were based on sites in the city, including allotments and some neighbouring farmland. Whatever the science or questionable interpretations of the science, the issue of soil health remains on the environmental agenda, and the proposals highlighted in the Agricultural Bill refer specifically to possible measures which reward farmers to manage their soils better.

But how can we measure these soil improvements? This would require a national soil-monitoring programme based on agreed factors which can be quantified easily. Can this be achieved to create an equitable assessment across hundreds of different soil types? This is one of the many uncertainties facing the roll-out of the new ELMS framework, described earlier. It is worth remembering this is UK taxpayers' money which will now be used to research the potential measure to be used, set up a monitoring programme, and ultimately pay the farmer. We can no longer blame the EU for farm payments we don't like. Can this national balancing act of promoting environmental concerns be carried out against the background of global issues such as a climate emergency, the potential for further pandemics, and an unstable international trading environment. More importantly, given the Covid-shaped hole in national budgets, what is realistically affordable?

These arguments are not new. In November 1988, the, Royal Society of Arts (RSA), brought together eminent scientists and others interested in the English landscape to discuss a 'Future Countryside Programme'. The issues raised by this well-informed audience is still pertinent three decades later. One issue addressed early in the conference was how much land Britain needs to produce food. The first speaker quoted studies from the 1960s, which concluded there was likely to be plenty of land available and indeed, there would be surplus land, with up to a third of agricultural available for other uses if the increase in productivity was maintained.[13]

In 1997, the Countryside Commission asked a scientific panel to look at the shape of the countryside and assess trends.[14] Their report lists the concerns of that time: farmers were unsure of their role; there were increasing demands for countryside access; and there was a danger that diversity in the landscape was being lost. Some twenty-five years later the uncertainty is still with us.

In any public debate involving land and its use, Britain is often described as, 'a crowded island': the idea of spare land, or moving away from the priority of food production, takes some time to absorb. However, these findings are in line with trends elsewhere in Europe. The future impact of agricultural and trade policy reform on land use across Europe brings into focus the issue of *land abandonment*. Estimates of this shrinkage of agricultural land have been made as the subsidy framework changes, support payments decline and the average age of the farming population creeps upwards. Overall, it is estimated that across Europe, around 8 per cent less land will be farmed under these reforms, with some regions and farm types facing more significant reductions. The reforms will be felt particularly on livestock grazing farms situated in the marginal areas of Europe. These areas, including Britain, also coincide with areas of high value for nature conservation.[15]

These trends move the discussion into the rarefied world of tariffs and standards, which will ultimately influence the prices the consumer is willing to pay for food, and equally importantly, the livelihoods of those producing for the export market. The maximum exposure then falls on livestock production, especially from less favourable farming regions, where the options for alternatives are limited. Often these are the most varied and scenic parts of Britain, such as the Cumbrian fells or the Welsh hills. Any additional costs to trade such as tariffs could result in a downturn in sheep and cattle from the hills, and perhaps the same decline in upland farming as elsewhere in mainland Europe. Margins for hill farmers are traditionally thin with an annual profit of less than £16,000 for the average upland sheep farm. Any increased costs are bound to increase the pressure, leading at worst to the abandonment of land, or an increase in the trend towards larger farming units. In addition, the average age of UK farmers is approaching 60 years and is likely older in traditional upland livestock-producing areas. Taken together, these factors point towards a fall in the labour force and a threat to a distinctive way of life.

The paradox in requiring areas such as the uplands of Britain to be protected in National Parks, and at the same time tilting the conditions for a making a livelihood away from profitability, is not lost on many who farm in these marginal areas and is well articulated in James Rebank's book, *The Shepherd's Life*. In his evocative description of the life of a Cumbrian shepherd, he bemoans the lack of understanding of the livelihoods of those working in this landscape. Operating a livestock business in such hostile environments is delicately poised and any adverse changes – in weather, subsidy, or fewer people eating meat – will have a rapid effect on farm budgets and keeping people working in these hill landscapes. The foot-and-mouth epidemic was a grim foretaste of this, removing rural tourism as a prop to the precious livelihoods of hill farming.

In a similar way, conversations around any changes in either environmental or food standards could curtail the market further. The farming industry in the UK has matched or exceeded food and animal welfare standards in the EU and beyond, and any move to weaken these in an attempt to agree comprehensive trade deals or lower food prices will have a direct impact on rural life. The National Farmers' Union (NFU) has made this point very strongly.

Trade, tariffs and tups

One of the most evocative descriptions in the account of Cumbrian shepherding by James Rebanks takes place in the spring, when the Herdwick rams or 'tups' are gathered from the fells for judging and sale. These events take place on traditional fields of lowland pasture close to Keswick, in Eskdale, and are much more than a simple business transaction. There is keen rivalry to display the best animals, achieve the highest prices and participate in a social occasion which has a long history. There is of course much discussion on markets and likely grumbles on prices. One future topic is likely to be the export trade to Europe and the potential impact of lamb imports into the UK, mostly from New Zealand.

The sheep trade operates on thin margins and any small adverse change in the terms of trade could have far-reaching consequence. Government spokespersons have repeated that the UK will not necessarily be bound by environmental or other standards adopted during its membership of the EU.[16] This could result in less rigorous rules on animal welfare – for example, during transport – which may then lead to difficulties with external markets, especially in Europe.

At the other end of this debate is the implied threat that food standards could be altered, allowing food imports into the UK which are cheaper, but which are presently illegal to trade within the UK. The UK Government can decide which rules to apply. The choices seem to be a high-welfare, premium-price livestock industry, or an acceptance that price is everything and, as a consequence, low import conditions and the undermining of domestic producers. The National Farmers Union is outspoken on this issue, with its president stating plainly that this is about national values not prices.[17] By mid-2020, a petition urging the Government to legislate to prevent imports of food produced in ways which are presently illegal in the UK had been signed by more than one million people.

Agricultural agreements with the US are of particular concern. Anticipating these challenges to the domestic standards, the Red Tractor scheme, created to promote British produce, has developed further to provide the consumer with more choice. The offering to consumers is now differentiated to include produce which is organic, or has met enhanced welfare standards or – in the case of poultry and pig meat – is free-range. The demand for organic produce continues to expand, with Waitrose recording a 13 per cent increase year on year in mid-2020.

The livestock industry has particular concerns, including the added pressure on markets from a gradual but persistent trend towards the consumption of less meat, the potential for wetter winters owing to global warming, and uncertainty over a new subsidy regime. Realistically, these difficulties could lead to a decline in animal husbandry across the UK uplands. Add to this lobbying from conservation groups to reduce the stocking levels on the fells and Welsh mountains, and they are valid concerns.[18]

So what level of payments is justified to support these rural livelihoods? How much do we want designated areas such as a National Park to be a working landscape, rather than an outdoor museum? Do we relate only to the landscape in these wilder areas, or can we also relate to the people who live there and take care of the landscape? In Cumbia, shepherds take enormous pride in producing a prize-winning Herdwick ram, as well as looking after their land.

To make the aspiration of 'nature-friendly farming' a reality, farmers and the larger landowners need to be convinced that subsidy systems will work and can be trusted. Can environmental measures be added to farm operations without reducing profitability? And better still, can this nature-friendly approach reduce costs, or at least happen without increased expenditure? Underlying this is a tension between farming and the environment which has been present for many generations. The EU Stewardship schemes began to chip away at this and many farms embraced it. During June 2020 the BBC early morning *Farming Today* programme covered the topic of wildlife and farming during a week of broadcasts, with stories of many farmers actively working towards an accommodation of commercial farming and the environment. Farmers who had gone well beyond the requirements of the Stewardship Agreements required to achieve funding, and who had restored meadows, planted new woodland and welcomed school parties, were all featured.

This chapter began with a review of food security and the prospects of UK feeding itself. For any government this is always a central priority. The 2020 pandemic further exposed the fragility of the UK food-security situation, with disruptions of overseas supply lines and the reliance on overseas workers in the agricultural sector causing alarm.

One possible outcome is a two-speed countryside with large – and they will need to be large – farms on the choice land, and low-intensity, or perhaps no farming at all, on less favourable terrain. The prospect is that spare land is then available for alternative use such as conservation. Alternatively, more effort could be made to persuade commercial farms to move towards the sharing of land with nature as part of any future incentive funding scheme. Such approaches require farm adaption in managing land for nature, as well as for crops and livestock. These are policy choices and the beginning of difficult political questions on the funding required; discussions that reach beyond the farming sector and into the political priorities of government funding.[19] All of these changes and a reset of farming support are dependent on building trust.

One topic is central to this debate: the future of small and mixed farms. The British ideal of the 'mixed farm' is increasingly rare and the future of small farms is problematical. How then do new farmers start their career, with the pressure to move to bigger units freezing out new entrants? In the past local authorities played a significant role by providing a ladder into the industry though County Farms' land units, which were usually small and available to rent.

Space for leisure

Bridle paths, now shared with off road cyclists, have always been integral to an intensively farmed landscape. In this photograph a rider uses a wide grassy headland flanked by a growing grain crop and a traditional hedge and ditch. This network of public paths allows valuable access to the countryside which is otherwise off limits. (Photograph by the author)

Starting at the bottom: smallholdings and county farms

Council-tax payers are mostly unaware that many local authorities throughout England still own and manage a farm estate. This is a long-standing arrangement, which was once seen as a useful role for local government to fulfil. Usually these farms are defined and described as 'smallholdings' and have been recognized in law since 1892. In the emergency food-security situation of the First World War, the Smallholdings Acts of 1916 and 1918 formalized this and, in 1919, the Land Settlement Act tapped into public sentiment and the idea that there was scope for a return to a yeoman class of smallholders to absorb ex-servicemen. There were also private schemes, which added to the quarter of a million acres bought by councils and supported around 25,000 families.

However, if you were to google the words, 'Council Farms' in 2020, the second site which is listed is, *'Council Farms for Sale'*. Further down the listing there is a more optimistic item leading to a report entitled, *'Reviving Council Farms'*. What has happened to the good intentions of providing a route into farming, with a small unit at an affordable rent? The answer is the squeeze on local-government finance, which has resulted in the sale of many Council Farms and, in some areas, the complete closure of the farm estate. Many of these small units attract high prices from housing developers, especially if positioned on the edge of a town, close to attractive countryside. The rents are intentionally low and the costs of operating the estate often high, so a hard-pressed local government finance officer needs convincing that there is a benefit from these farm holdings. Council or County Farms are regarded like a local library or leisure centre – something that can be disposed of. The bleak conclusion is that these are seen as a leftover from the past.

In 2019, the Council for the Protection of Rural England (CPRE) issued a report, which expressed dismay that this valued public resource was being 'slowly leached away'. Across England, a quarter of all local authorities have sold farms since 2010. During the years of austerity, this loss sped up alarmingly and over the past forty years the area of the publicly owned farm estate has halved.[20]

Some local authorities have resisted the trend and been clear that these farms: offer an opportunity for rural education; increase access to the countryside; provide areas for tree-planting; and in a few places, operate as 'care farms', specializing in providing disadvantaged or disabled young people with a supervised outdoor experience. In the wider context, the provision of small starter farms, where skills can be tried and apprenticeships served, is more than ever a requirement as the move to larger commercial units gathers pace and opportunities for young farmers are squeezed.

In general, once people are aware of these farms there is support for their retention. Central Bedfordshire Council (CBC) carried out a consultation which showed these units were valued if they could be made to work, which resulted in the Council adopting what has been described as a *proactive* approach to management. Nevertheless, there is a desire to rationalize the estate, which will mean sales in the order of £5 million in the next five years.

At the other end of this scale, the tendency of commercial farms to be concentrated in large management units, with efficiency and production the priority, is now well established. Presently, all farms both large and small collect the basic area farm payment and many also incorporate basic environmental requirements, which allow the payment at the enhanced level of stewardship agreements. But how far can these commercial units can combine production, yield-optimization and profitability with a nature-friendly approach to farming?

The intention of this book is not to deliver pat answers, but to unravel some of the questions which will soon impact the British countryside and might become central to future discussion over our relationship with landscape and nature. At the heart of this is the understanding that, across the UK, the landscape we see in the countryside today is 75 per cent farmed land. This is the result of endeavour and investment by countless people over time. Since the first clearances were made in the wildwood following the retreat of ice, the urge to act as a steward and land-improver has taken on deep roots. This applies as much to the stone walls of the Yorkshire Dales as it does to the hydraulically engineered fens of Cambridgeshire. How much are we willing to change or protect these landscapes?

As the NFU has argued, this is as much a *moral*, or at least a *value* question as it is about economics. But how much land do we need for active farming? And can a rural economy be sustained without farming as the main industry? To maintain its presence, we need a workable and well-financed framework of subsidies as envisioned by Government in the new proposals. Funds for this will now come direct from the UK tax base rather than through the Brussels Administration and this then sets farm payments against other funding demands: health, schools, jobs ... and HS2.

What is the optimum level of subsidy and what is this subsidy for? With UK agriculture only contributing 0.5 per cent to the national economy is there scope for change? What level of food security should the UK aim for and how much land is required to produce this?

Chapter 2 opens up this discussion about the land that is not farmed and which could be planted with trees.

CHAPTER TWO

Planting the Right Tree in the Right Place

There is one wood which is called Heyle which contains fourscore acres and another called Litlelund which contains thirty-two acres ... (From *The Ely Coucher Book,* 1251)[1]

The quote above is one of many records of specific English woods in medieval manuscripts. Woods were valued assets and therefore managed, measured and recoded in legal documents. The Domesday Book, for example, records the capacity of woods to sustain a pig herd: in Bedfordshire the wood at Millbrook was judged adequate to support 100 pigs, whereas in nearby Ampthill the figure is 300 swine. Using these records, it is possible to estimate the extent of the tree cover at around 15 per cent of England at the time of the Domesday Survey in 1086.

During the UK election campaign of 2019, the pledges on tree-planting became an important issue, taking electioneering into very different political territory. Woodlands were part of all the political parties' manifesto offerings, as efforts to combat climate change gathered pace. At times the political noise around the campaign resembled a bidding war.[2] The Labour Party opened with a pledge of tree-planting at a rate of 60 million trees every year from 2020 to 2025, reaching around 2 billion new trees by 2040, bringing the UK tree cover to 25 per cent. The Conservative offering was 30 million trees a year until 2025, bringing the national cover to over 16 per cent of the land cover. These figures were debated against the backdrop of the Committee on Climate Change (CCC) estimate, which analysed the part played by woodland in meeting the Government's target of net zero carbon emissions by 2050. The CCC suggested increasing UK woodland cover from its current low level of 13 per cent of total land cover to at least 17 per cent, given that ideally 19 per cent of UK land cover by 2050 would be required to make any contribution to the carbon-reduction target.

Friends of the Earth were more ambitious. They had confidence that the UK had the land available for this expansion of woodland, the snag being that it would require a reduction in our consumption of meat and dairy over time, with land use altered from pasture to woodland. Even the doubling of woodland cover from today's levels will still leave the UK behind many other countries: the current European average woodland cover is 38 per cent. In the 2020 March budget, the Chancellor began to provide some detail of what was proposed by announcing a 'Nature for Climate Fund', which pledged £640 million over five years, which he suggested was adequate to plant 30,000 hectares (ha) of land (around 115 square miles) by 2025. This figure of 30,000 ha is important as the CCC suggested this would be required every year until 2050, in order to approach the target on atmospheric carbon reduction.[3] However, the scale of this planting is formidable. In England, during the financial year 2018–19, only around

£5.2 million of Government funding was spent on tree-planting, with a mere 1,300 ha planted.[4] In the face of these practical difficulties the promised *England Tree Strategy* will report later in 2020.[5]

Whatever way these numbers are viewed, these pledges are significant in that the planting of new woodland is seen as a benefit and a 'public good'. The Government seems to have committed to a significant area of Britain being turned over to woodland: trees are on the political agenda and this has the potential to change the face of the countryside. The most extreme woodland-planting forecast figures would then far exceed the medieval tree cover of 15 per cent for England estimated back in 1086. This fell dramatically during the expansion of agriculture until the mid-14th century, when the Black Death began to make inroads into rural life. The implication for the targets set by politicians is that tree cover could return to the level of coverage of before Roman occupation.

During late 2019 and the early months of 2020, two main concerns came together to drive this political conversion towards trees and woodlands. There was an alarming quickening of the pace of climate change, which during 2019 was catapulted into the political arena with the Extinction Rebellion demonstrations catching the public mood. Despite the critics focusing on the tactics used, the imagination of young people worldwide was fired and politicians could no longer ignore the issue. As this is a complex scientific debate the easy political response was to reach for an easy remedy – plant trees – hence the sudden appearance of forestry in the 2019 election debates.

By early 2020, the simple equation of 'More trees = Less carbon dioxide' was being challenged by scientists. Although there was an acceptance that the planting of woodlands in Britain remains important to reduce carbon dioxide in the atmosphere, there are still important choices remaining.[6]

Tree mania or pragmatic response to climate change?

This interconnection of tree-planting and a reduction in carbon has taken some time to register. In 2007, the Parliamentary Office for Science and Technology published a briefing note entitled *UK Trees and Forests*, in which no mention was made of the role of trees in the storage of carbon from the atmosphere, and the topic of climate change was limited to a few sentences on the impact of changing temperature on new pests and tree diseases.[6] A decade later trees were seen as the primary agent in combatting what was being referred to as a 'climate emergency', and the Government response was to launch a £50 million scheme to boost the rate of tree-planting across Britain in an attempt to combat climate change. The Government briefing on the new funding arrangement explains that such a scheme would give land managers the long-term financial incentive needed to invest in carbon storage: trees are seen as a 'nature-based solution' to climate change.[7]

This attraction to trees is explained by the botanical fact that all plants, including trees, absorb carbon dioxide from the atmosphere, thus removing a major source of one greenhouse gas responsible for climate change. Trees are especially important as their life cycle is relatively long in relation to crops or pasture. Additionally, the soil in a woodland builds up a store of organic material many times greater than that under arable crops. At the moment, UK forests are estimated to remove 10 million tonnes of this greenhouse gas and the aspiration is to double this.[8] However, by early 2020, concerns were being raised as to the practicality of achieving these optimistic tree-planting goals, and there was a real danger of poor decisions being taken in the rush to simply get the trees in the ground. The problems which emerged included: the source of the saplings; the surprisingly skilled labour needed to plant them properly; the requirement for a long-term view of the investment made in new woodlands; and, importantly, the areas of land required. The deep-rooted view that trees will thrive on the leftover corners of land in Britain not used for agriculture will need to be rethought. How will decisions be made on the amount and quality of land to be converted into new woods?

The temptation to plant and walk away needs to be resisted. Young saplings are fragile and prone to drought, high winds, deer and rabbits, and vandalism. It is estimated that a quarter of all new trees could die on some sites.

There is the sobering thought that ambitious targets have a habit of proving counterproductive. Tree saplings or whips cannot be made to order in a 'just-in-time' supply line. Often these saplings are imported, usually from the Netherlands. If the intention is to use native seed this needs to be collected, and nursery facilities set up and provided with some assurances on future contacts. The risks are high:

estimates during the pandemic were that 10 million trees were destroyed as there was no labour to plant them, and the aftercare required is often underestimated. There will be more bonfires of trees if targets are missed.[9]

A Woodland Carbon Code, launched as the gold standard for new plantings in 2011, aimed to ensure that new woodlands were certified and had reliable carbon sequestration levels estimated. This is a voluntary standard for woodland creation projects and includes factors such as when the trees will be thinned or felled, and how the site is restocked with trees to ensure the permanence of the carbon storage beyond one planting cycle. An important point stressed by the Carbon Trust is that broadleaf species such as oak and beech pay out the greatest carbon dividends in the long run, and have the added benefit of being best for biodiversity.[10]

Despite the pushback on the direct effectiveness of tree-planting in the storage of carbon, the consensus seems to be that trees are an effective means of combatting both climate change and the depletion of biodiversity across British landscapes. The idea of tree-planting has proved very effective in engaging people, especially children. As an environmental message, it is easy to sell. This does not mean a simplistic rush to plant trees will always be effective. There will be examples of the wrong tree in the wrong place and disappointing rates of sapling survival. There is also the concern that tree-planting simply deflects the focus onto the overall effort to reduce emissions; that trees are an effective 'greenwash' for corporate business and governments.

As the scientific evidence on effectiveness continues to grow, certain themes run through all the reporting on this topic: the importance of involving local people in planting; and the understanding that one benefit from new woods is improved public access. Simply converting large blocks of land into forest will not win any friends, as demand for an outdoor experience, especially walking and off-road cycling, continues to gain momentum.

The debate over increased woodland cover has raised many questions and any rush to plant new and extensive woodlands will require careful thought over the choices needed to achieve the correct balance. These choices often pull in different directions. The best example is the alternative of fast-growing conifers, and what are usually described as 'mixed broadleaf plantations'. Conifers grow quickly, tolerate difficult conditions of wetness and wind, and survive on poor upland soils. It is no accident that the dominant tree planted on the British uplands by foresters in the 1970s was the ubiquitous Sitka spruce, a native of tough unwelcoming conditions in Alaska, and western Canada. The 1970s' spread of uniform conifer plantations across upland Britain is now questioned by foresters and environmentalists. On the peat landscapes in Scotland, such as the extensive area of deep peat known as the 'Flow Country' of Caithness and Sutherland, the trees failed and the new plantations did little for biodiversity. Endangered species such as the curlew, an iconic bird of the uplands, suffered a decline. The social pressures on rural life, with large swathes of conifer-only plantations, have not helped with a retreat from marginal land in areas of upland Wales and Scotland. The counter argument is that fast-growing conifers have a valuable part to play in providing a much-needed timber supply, which can be a replacement for the concrete and steel responsible for substantial carbon emissions.

Another reason that renewed interest in woodlands caught the public mood was a bundle of other issues which could loosely be grouped under environmental conservation, including improved air quality, the amelioration of flooding, increased biodiversity and public access. For several decades, there has been a steady drip of news which reinforces the intuitive public feeling that all is not well with the environment. The realization that air quality was declining and causing increased death rates was a very clear signal, as was the yearly surveys on farmland birds, which demonstrated alarming gaps in what had been common species. Also, diseases in common tree species such as ash dieback and concern over pollinators all fed into rising public concern.

A home for dormice – Maulden Woods

Maulden Woods are well known locally for spring bluebells but less known as a site selected for the release of the endangered dormouse as part of English Natures' recovery programme. Dormice have now begun to spread beyond the wood. These woods are a Site of Special Scientific Interest and are managed by Forestry England. (Photograph by Richard Revels)

Tiny forests in the city

A space big enough for a 'tiny forest'

There is a strong compulsion for people to plant trees and this takes many forms. One of most intriguing to emerge is a movement to plant very small patches of land densely and with a variety of tree species, in places that are not usually considered part of any designated nature area. The *tiny* forests can be the size of six parking spaces or perhaps a tennis court, and are found alongside roads and in school playgrounds. This idea began with a Japanese biologist, Akira Miyawaki, some fifty years ago, and has spread across Asia to Europe, where researchers at the Dutch University of Wageningen have been monitoring the results. One hundred of these forests have been planted in the Netherlands since 2015, and the idea is taking root in Belgium and France: the first UK tiny forest has been planted in Whitney, Oxfordshire, and others are now planned in the county.

The Whitney forest will have around 600 trees on 200 square metres; a mix of species, including oak, birch and blackthorn trees.[12]

Throughout the last decade the language has changed and the emphasis has moved to now explain trees and woodland as essential parts of what are now viewed as 'ecological services'. This approach to a new way of thinking underlies the Environment Bill (2019–20), and Government has reached out to farmers and landowners to stress that scientists are evaluating these natural resources and habitats, and then making the evidence available in a user-friendly way. Ideas have been made accessible in an online resource set up by government called 'Enabling a Natural Capital Approach', which is designed to bring evidence together in one place.[11] Farming columns in the regional press have begun to engage with weighty terms such as 'natural capital', and the notional values placed on riverside meadows or a small patch of woodland.

More than just the trees

As mentioned, the Domesday Book provided details of woods owned by estate holders in 1086, and these were given a value according to the number of pigs the patch of woodland could sustain. The swine herd became the measure of value. Attention then moved on from the estimates of pigs to the usefulness of timber to medieval villagers for the production of poles and oak beams. In the eighteenth century England was concerned about timber supply for ships, and naval officers on shore leave were asked to distribute acorns on country estates. By the mid-twentieth century, woodland was only assigned a value estimated to be equivalent to the area of land which could then be turned over to farming, with the timber only a minor financial value concern.

Today, a modern resource economist might be more interested in the biodiversity of the woods and be challenged to place a value on the visitor attraction, the rarity of the woodland plants or the bat population. The woodland would then be seen as a 'multifaceted environmental asset', which offers environmental services: timber production, flood protection, leisure outlet, biodiversity reserve, repository for carbon, or perhaps a place to graze rare-breed pigs or wild boar! Ecological services are best described as the benefits such habitats provide to making human life both possible and worth living. Woodlands have become a 'public good' and given an economic value as a provider of services to the environment.

In order to accommodate the diversity of these ecological services it is best to think in terms of three groups. First, there are tangible benefits, such as the wood or the timber yield which can be measured in volume, or the less valuable wood sold to fuel a wood-burning stove. Second are the benefits which are more difficult to measure, such as the storing of carbon from the atmosphere; the offering of some protection against floods downstream; or filtering the air, which is seen as an increasingly important asset close to roads. Third, there are what are loosely described as 'cultural services', such as a place to walk or run, for children to build dens, for artists to paint the bluebells and for spiritual renewal.

Coppiced woods at Moggerhanger

The management of woodland, long neglected has been revived with conservation agencies, now practicing the techniques of coppicing as illustrated.

If we accept that all these services are real then the next clear step asks whether these can all be valued in monetary terms. This is more than saying, 'This is a beautiful wood, an ancient wood, and lovely with bluebells in the spring'. For many the argument that it is possible to place a value on nature is false, offensive and unethical.[13] More practically, the economic equation is exceedingly difficult and full of assumptions which are open to challenge. A simple example is when a piece of woodland is open and free to the public and then a charge is introduced for access to it, or more likely, for parking. How much are people willing to pay to visit and how often? To complicate the argument, the context of a wood is important. Does a wood on the edge of London have more potential leisure value than in well-wooded Nottinghamshire?

This public concern is often brought into focus by the removal of what are described as 'ancient forests'. This terminology is used to describe woodland which existed before 1600, when reliable mapping became widespread. In 1664, John Evelyn (1620–1706), published the first known book on English forestry, which for the first time paid attention to planting trees rather than simply cutting a wood for timber. Only around 2 per cent of these ancient forests still stand and these are not only important historically and scientifically, as they contain plant communities which are now rare, but they also usually have interesting man-made features, such as medieval boundary markers, historic charcoal-burning sites and are especially peaceful and beautiful places, valued by the public. These are the much-visited woods with woodpeckers drumming and bluebells in the spring.

The threat to these woodlands was once again highlighted as the HS2 rail-line construction moved ahead. With the implementation of HS2, around sixty ancient woods will suffer partial destruction and this will be compensated by new planting. This idea is that the planting of approximately 7 million trees and shrubs, creating over 3,000 ha of new habitat for wildlife, will compensate for any disruption. Ecologists however are not convinced. One particular concern is the bizarre idea that the soil from the older wood can simply be dug out and then dumped in a new location to effectively mimic the ancient forest.

Kilometres of fungal strands and billions of bacteria

In order to reduce the potential damage caused by infrastructure development on ancient woodland sites, it has been suggested that the wood can simply be moved. This proposal seems to occur in development proposals and has received much critical comment in the context of the HS2 proposals in the Midlands. The term is 'translocation' and is used to describe a mix of new plantings and the physical moving of trees, undergrowth and, most importantly, soils to a new location. Five sites were suggested initially for this treatment, with the aim of doubling the area of the original disturbed woodland, but in a new location. In 2013, the Woodland Trust carried out a systematic assessment of the possibility of translocating habitats and reviewed the evidence. In regard to moving ancient woodland their conclusions were clear:

Some habitats may be successfully translocated in toto, but these would be transient and highly dynamic habitats, and ancient woodland does not fall within this category. There is no evidence that stable climax communities, such as ancient woodland, can be recreated though habitat translocation, and current policy guidance is that it cannot.[14]

The arguments have focused around the moving or translocation of woodland soils, which have developed over long time periods, in situ. A vivid, non-scientific explanation is a good description of the problems of digging up and moving a body of soil:

This stuff is alive. There is life you can see — earthworms, and skinny centipedes, fragments of roots and shoots — and life you cannot: kilometres of fungal hyphae in every handful, thousands of nematodes, billions of bacteria.[15]

These soils are an outcome of the long-term management of the woods across Britain, which has been invested in by generations over many centuries. The time scales are so lengthy that there is great uncertainty over the ecological processes which combine to make up a woodland habitat. Faced with the immovable development of a major government-backed infrastructure project, the best word to use when dealing with woodland is 'salvage'. There seems slim chance of the rapid re-establishment of the woodland. Shakespeare had the idea: 'Bring me no more reports. Let them fly all. Till Birnam wood remove to Dunsinane' *Macbeth*: V, iii).

Recent advances in the biology of woodland have taken this notion to a new level in Peter Wohlleben's book, *The Hidden Life of Trees: What They Feel, How They Communicate – Discoveries from a Secret World.* As the title suggests, this popular text explores how trees in a wood communicate, and how a woodland is an interdependent community of species. This has been a previously little-understood world into which Wohlleben brings scientific understanding of the complete web of woodland life, including the life of roots and soils.[16] Another perception has been added by Sarah Maitland in *Gossip from the Forest*: *The Tangled Roots of our Forests and Fairytales,* which points out the important role played by woodland in folklore, fairy tales and literature.[17]

One success story of increasing woodland has been the re-establishment of the National Forest in the English Midlands: the land of the ancient Sherwood Forest. Over a period of 25 years woodland cover has increased from 6 per cent to over 20 per cent. Two key ingredients have ensured the success of this new venture. Firstly, there has been the building of strong partnerships, including government at both local and national levels, environmental groups, education charities, landowners and farmers, local business and housing developers – and most importantly, the public. The careful formation of this consensus required as much time, effort and funding as the physical planting of trees.

Secondly, this is far from dense uniform forest. The area of the National Forest includes farms, new homes, small towns and local business enterprises and more than a 250,000 people live there. The forest evolved as part of a plan that thought about the landscape as much as the trees, and the decisions made now will impact the land in fifty years' time.

The medieval idea of a wood as pasture for pigs, a timber supply, a source of fuel and a larder of last resort in time of shortage are all reflected in ancient legal documents, which ensured that woodland had a real value in rural livelihoods. These ideas are now being re-appraised as woodland is viewed as a provider of many and varied ecological services in the twenty-first century. We now attach value to woodland for different aspects of life, such as flood prevention, a refuge for biodiversity, to help with cleaner air, or simply as a place to walk, run or cycle. Woods are best understood as part of a healthy landscape mosaic: an idea which would have been very familiar to a fourteenth-century swineherd.

If the pledges of tree-planting at scale come to fruition, the increased area of woodland will have the greatest visual impact on the countryside since the enclosure of open fields in the early nineteenth century. The direct benefits for wildlife, the environment and the storage of carbon are now well understood and the indirect effects on air quality and downstream flooding are becoming more significant as the climate warms. If this increased woodland can be combined with greater access, then the public will become enthusiastic supporters and make full use of new opportunities to enjoy trees in all seasons of the year. There is a public appetite for trees and woods and an opportunity at the beginning of a new decade to enhance the landscape. If the reality is that measuring and giving an economic value to a wood, then this will be increasingly accepted as necessary to secure the changes needed in bringing about a well wooded landscape.

Ensuring that future woodland planting schemes take into account a variety of final objectives, beyond simply planting saplings trees in great numbers, is what we turn to next. The following chapters explore these environmental and human connections. beginning with the disastrous depletion of habitats in which wildlife can flourish.

CHAPTER THREE

Of Hedgehogs and Hedges

Some twenty years ago a family of hedgehogs lived under our garden shed, to the delight of the children and the bewilderment of the cat, who spent many hours sitting at the shed door. In contrast, our grandchildren have never seen a hedgehog, which to them is an animal from a bedtime picture book, as remote as a snow leopard. Like the disappearance of the skylarks from the local fields, this decline in hedgehog numbers should not come as a surprise. In July 2020 hedgehogs were added to the UK red list of endangered species, joining more exotic species such as the Scottish wildcat. Numbers in the countryside have fallen by a half or more since 2000, and road-kill figures are estimated at over 100,000 each year.[1]

In contrast, hedgehog numbers were estimated at 36 million in Britain in the 1950s. At the local level of the suburban garden, this decline in hedgehog numbers is noticeable and immediate, and makes the point that there is a significant change underway in the natural world, impacting as much on towns as across the countryside. Conservation organizations attempt to explain the causes for this sudden decline as a combination of the widespread use of pesticides, resulting in a decline in insect numbers, together with the loss of hedgerows and the removal of permanent pasture. In general, rural hedgehogs are not doing well as agriculture intensifies … which brings us to hedgerows.

A hedged, veined landscape

The story of the hedgerow in the agriculture of lowland England is long and often simplified into a tale of doom as hedges began to disappear from the landscape.[2] The lowland hedge, usually of hawthorn and flanked by a ditch, reached its greatest extent following the enclosure movement of the late eighteenth and early nineteenth centuries. A new system of agriculture demanded fields which could be managed as individual units, and so the hedge was the most essential part of this transformed landscape of regular and tidy fields which came to define the countryside, notably in England.

Hedges are a sign of a managed landscape: they assert ownership of the land, allow livestock to be controlled, and in the past, separated the farmed from the wild. Estimates for England are that the total length of hedges almost tripled during the period of enclosure, as regular, managed fields replaced the open-field landscape that had dominated the land from the arrival of Saxon farmers in the sixth century. Swathes of common land essential to the livelihood of rural people were enclosed, accelerating the drift from the countryside to the town. The granting of the right to enclose an estate came with the requirement for a boundary to be maintained. The hedging plant of choice was the hawthorn, aptly named 'quick', to denote the speed at which hawthorn established a stock-proof barrier. During the nineteenth century, advertisements in newspapers, in counties such as Leicestershire, carried notices of tenders for the supply of many thousands of quick hedging plants.

Although hedges seem a natural part of the landscape, the majority are man-made and need to be managed. Ignore a hedge and it will become a line of trees. Isabella Tree, in her book Wilding, describes in colourful language what happened on the Knepp Estate in Sussex, when the land and hedges were abandoned and returned to nature: 'Miles of hedgerows, previously flailed every autumn, now exploded into the welcoming humus, billowing out like a dowager loosening her stays.'[3]

The ancient craft of hedge-laying to discipline a hedge has enjoyed a revival, with classes in the best techniques and competitions common across the country. There are over thirty regional styles of hedge-laying known throughout Britain, each distinctive and immediate to the locality.

Hedges have been called the 'veins' in the landscape, offering corridors for wildlife, linking habitats. The hedge is the refuge for vital crop pollinators, as well as a source of berries and nuts for farmland birds, and older hedges retain an important reservoir of rare plants. In drier summers hedges play a part in exposed sites, preventing the removal of top soil by wind, and in the winter and the cold spring months, offer shelter to livestock. Hedges are in many landscapes the most abundant semi-natural habitat and as such are useful for educational study. Finally, hedges, as the name suggests, are the natural home of the much-loved hedgehog and also badgers (less loved by cattle farmers).

Agricultural cycles of boom and bust before and after the First World War did not impact greatly on the pattern of hedges in the countryside, but this picture changed rapidly after 1950. The clamour to end rationing and the national demand for a secure food supply made feeding a population the priority for any government. The arrival of American-made caterpillar-tracked tractors during the Second World War placed new and powerful tools in the hands of farming contractors and, aided by government subsidy, hedgerows and ancient woodlands were an early casualty. Larger farm machinery and increased mechanization generally demanded larger field sizes. Hedges were grubbed up at that time and ancient woodlands endured a worse fate, with contractors paid at a piece-work rate to remove each tree. There was a love affair with roads and emerging motorways, and along the route of the M1 around thirty woods were felled. The national concern over food security was captured by an observation from a farm in Cheshire, noted by Derek Neimann:

Once a month a friendly face appeared on the scene. He was the well-spoken man from Ministry and he was there to help. He was very keen on maximising everything. They just wanted food, food, food.[4]

Hedgerows have been so much a part of the landscape of Britain that it was not until the 1980s that the realization that these were under threat was more widely understood. There are many statistics which have attempted to measure the loss, with much of the information conflicting. The pressure to increase food production required larger farms, bigger fields and more advanced machinery: hedges were in the way.

The value of hedges was formally recognized in 1997, when a change in the law meant that the removal of a hedge needed to have a well-documented, specific reason. Agricultural Stewardship Agreements rewarded hedge-planting with enhanced subsidy payments. In addition, there has been a steady and welcome recognition that hedges not only add character and interest to the landscape, but are also important for biodiversity and wildlife. It is estimated that today, some 250,000 miles of hedgerows are looked after by farmers in England, with new plantings of just over 18,000 miles in the last twenty years.

***

The issue of hedges and indeed of hedgehogs is a useful example of the countryside dilemma. For the commercial farmer, removing a hedge or replacing it with a post-and-wire fence gives more flexibility, releases more land and might reduce the infestation of pests. For the conservationist, the hedge line is a linear routeway for wildlife in the countryside, a source of food for farmland birds, and its removal diminishes a significant habitat. For the casual countryside-user, such as the walker or rambler, the removal of the hedge often means the headland footpath is reduced to a narrow path, alongside a wire fence that crosses an arable field, which is a much less pleasant experience.

This is the argument posed in Chapter 1, whereby *public goods for public funds* is now the accepted policy for any future agricultural subsidy, followed by the dilemma of how far the balance can be tilted away from the production of food. If this is the future, then how much land can be spared for non-commercial non-farming use, and how best can the environment be protected? Should nature be confined to the edges of land left at farming margins, or should we place conservation more centrally in the land use of the farmed and productive countryside?

In 2010, the ecologist Professor John Lawton set out the dire situation facing wildlife and nature throughout the UK. His report also provided a preceptive pathway out of this perilous decline in both plant and animal species.[5] Government seemed to take note of this detailed and sober scientific audit of the state of wildlife, and a year later the Secretary of State for the Environment, Caroline Spelman, tabled a White Paper, which explicitly linked a healthy environment with public health. The title of the Government document reflected this – *Natural Choice: Securing the Value of Nature* – and this Government statement went on to state boldly that, 'this Government wants to be the first generation to leave the environment in a better state than it inherited'.[6]

Despite these well-intentioned Government policy statements, the picture for wildlife at the start of a new decade, is bleak and well-summarized by Mark Cocker in *Our Place: Can we save Britain's Wildlife before it is too late?*[7] As the title suggests, this book is an alarm call – one of many – which tries to set out clearly the gravity of the present position across the countryside. When we have Government ministers saying the same thing, then perhaps it is time to take notice. Michael Gove, in a speech in July 2019, said that: 'The United Kingdom is now among the most nature-depleted nations in the world'.[8]

The former Secretary of State, was speaking at Kew Gardens to an international gathering of scientists and was forthright in setting out the challenge in England and Wales. The picture he described will be recognized by many: the loss of about 97 per cent of wildflower meadows in England and Wales since the 1930s; and since the 1970s, a decline of over half our farmland-bird indicator species, with some individual species falling by over 90 per cent. Overall, more UK species declined than grew between 2002 and 2013.

The message as delivered is therefore stark: 'nature is slipping away from these islands; slowly, steadily, field by field, dyke by dyke'.[9]

A good place to begin grappling with this decline is a series of sobering reports, which encapsulate the Government's own audit of the overall state of wildlife, conservation and biodiversity in England. The Lawson Report of 2010 was followed by an invaluable series of three 'State of Nature' reports, published in 2013, 2016 and 2019.[10]

Charting the decline: the state of nature across England

The 2010 Lawton Report set out the argument for action to reverse the steep decline in the status of British wildlife. In the Executive Summary to his report, Professor Lawton asked a very simple question:

Do England's wildlife sites comprise a coherent and resilient ecological network? If not, what needs to be done?[11]

The answer was equally simple: nature was in trouble, and the protection being offered was inadequate. What was required, he referred to as a 'step-change in nature conservation'. Building on the extensive records of species and observations, he charted a steady decline in the number of species across the countryside and was especially concerned with the provisions which existed in 2010 for conservation and protection; in particular, the network of designated and protected sites such as Sites of Special Scientific Interest (SSSIs). He concluded that: many of these sites were not in good condition; they were too small to be effective; they were not connected in any way and therefore were only islands of protection; and finally, there were simply not enough protected sites across England to make a difference. Summarizing in carefully chosen conclusions, he called for more sites, which were larger, better maintained, and joined to others. Lawton issued a clear warning a decade ago - we needed to *'make space for nature'*, which then became the title of his influential report.

In the decade which followed, this message was repeated, beginning with a series of *State of Nature* reports in 2013. All make depressing reading. In response to the 2019 report, the National Trust produced a document with a title which echoes the despair that the damage was becoming irreversible: *State of Nature 2019: UKs wildlife loss continues unabated.*[12] This 2019 report found that no real improvements had been made since the survey in 2016. Agricultural land-use change was identified as the main contributing factor, with the increasing impacts of climate warming, pollution, growing urban development and invasive species all adding to the pressure on nature and wildlife. These reports draw on exhaustive but disparate records, which can be pulled together into a scientific value known as the 'Biological Intactness Index', which provides a unified assessment of how nature is surviving and allows international comparisons. As Mark Cocker remarked, it makes for uncomfortable reading, with the UK becoming one of the world's most nature-depleted countries.

Many environmental campaigners have pointed out the paradox as the UK overall has a significant number of people not only interested in wildlife and nature conservation, but willing to spend time and money on efforts to foster and protect the environment. The large national conservation organizations such as the National Trust and the Royal Society for the Protection of Birds (RSPB) are at the top of a hierarchy of many small and specialist charities devoted to the welfare of everything from butterflies and bats to barn owls. The numbers are revealing. The 2019 membership of the National Trust was 5.6 million with an income of £634 million, a rise of £40 million on the previous year. There are voluntary groups involved in the regular collection of data, and universities researching all aspects of the environment. So why the gap between this public interest and such a downward spiral of nature throughout the UK?

There is an inescapable conclusion from these reports and scientific audits: nature and wildlife in Britain are in trouble and piecemeal efforts to restore any sense of a recovery will need government leadership, changes in agricultural policy, the cooperation of the many conservation organizations, public support and understanding, and lots of money. Can we parcel wildlife into neat reserves and hope this is adequate? One alternative is to work towards *nature-friendly* farming backed by a radical support framework delivered through subsidies. Another is to be very radical and embrace new ideas of wilding or *re*wilding, which allow nature to take over in defined areas, with all the consequences of quite dramatic changes to the appearance of the countryside.

A nation addicted to tidiness, or ready for a wilder Britain?

Records of the last wild beaver in England can be traced back to 1526, when hunting for both fur and castoreum, a valued ingredient of perfumes, wiped out the native population. However, by 2008, the Eurasian beaver was back on the River Otter in Devon. There is no clear understanding of who released these animals or when this happened. However, following complaints from anglers, the animals were captured and a trial was undertaken prior to a supervised future release in estates in Cornwall, Cumbria, Norfolk and Sussex. Now a pair or more of beavers are the 'must-have' animals for large estates which are open to visitors: beavers are now a wildlife attraction.[13] These new introductions require a licence and in Scotland, which has moved more quickly, there are now thriving populations in the Tay River system in the east and Knapdale in the west. The beaver was recognized as a protected species in 2016.

Beavers are at the fashionable end of the nature-recovery movement, which in more radical forms is often referred to as either, 'rewilding' or simply 'wilding'. In England the 1,400-ha Knepp Estate has led the way, and Isabella Tree used the term, 'wilding' as the title of her 2018 book, which traces the fascinating account of moving away from conventional farming and turning the difficult clay land of a Sussex estate over to nature, and allowing natural processes to take the lead.[14] This was a landscape-scale experiment which recognized that small isolated nature reserves would never be satisfactory in redressing the balance of a decline in wildlife. Ecologists have come to recognize that, to be effective, conservation needs to be tackled on a scale beyond the limited space of a single nature reserve.

Radical groups throughout Europe have attempted to jump-start the return to wildlife with 'wilding projects', which reach well beyond the introduction of a pair of beavers. The pioneers at a Dutch polder site not far from Amsterdam demonstrated that the introduction of large mammals such as native-breed pigs stirred up the surface vegetation, thus hastening the return of insects and birds. These initiatives are not always welcome. Elsewhere, attempts to re-introduce lynx to the wilder areas of Northumberland have been vetoed by shepherds and there are persistent reports of beavers being shot in Scotland despite protection.[15] In Bedfordshire the return of otters to both the Great Ouse and smaller streams has been generally welcomed, although with less enthusiasm by anglers.

Established nature conservation organizations have set about the task of acquiring land, such as the Great Fen project in East Anglia. This then allows conservation, which is carefully managed and operates at a landscape scale. In other locations more modest wilding projects are underway. The National Trust has taken tentative steps to return the Ennerdale Valley in the Lake District to a wilder state, by removing the boundary fences separating forest from pasture and encouraging the natural regeneration of broadleaf trees.[16] New ideas are springing to life all over Britain; for example, an attempt to launch the community purchase of a former grouse moorland close to the border town of Langholm, Scotland, an area that already has some SSSIs. The challenge is to boost the wildlife and encourage a range of habitats.

The thorn is the mother of the oak

Opposition to wilding, or more often rewilding, usually comes when larger mammals are released into the countryside: fishermen complain about beavers; shepherds are adamant that sea eagles or lynx are incompatible with sheep-rearing; and ramblers are terrified of meeting a wild boar on a public footpath. However, there is space for the less controversial aspects of wilding to encourage red squirrels, for instance, or the return of native forest. Isabella Tree, in describing the return of woodland to the Knepp Estate, underlines the value of scrub regeneration to allow trees such as oak to be re-established. Although the appeal of the spade in planting a new tree sapling is immediate, it takes patience and the ability to withstand the critics and allow thorny scrub to take over previously tidy arable fields. She also advocated larger grazing animals such as wild cattle to act as browsers to tackle the tougher vegetation. These ideas have been taken up in Kent, where the local Wildlife Trust and a conservation charity, the Wildwood Trust, have secured an agreement to introduce four European bison into carefully fenced enclosures in Blean Woods in 2021. These large animals have been described as *ecosystem engineers* and will radically alter the ground vegetation and create a more varied habitat. It will be the first time bison have roamed across any part of Britain since the early melting of the last ice covering, around 15,000 years ago. In Europe, the species was hunted into extinction in the 1920s.[17]

In tandem with these changes such as the stocking of large herbivores, allowing the former neat hedges to expand and double in size has greatly encouraged increased natural tree cover. This will change the appearance of the countryside and directly challenges our notion of arable fields and parklands with peacefully grazing domestic livestock. The potential for the parkland landscapes of Britain to fulfil a greatly enhanced role in the conservation of rare habitats is now being actively explored, with exciting possibilities for a wilder but less 'tidy' Britain.

Results from these wilding experiments have been amazing and have had immediate public appeal. The Purple Emperor butterfly has appeared in numbers at Knepp and is moving into urban gardens, and in 2020, white stork chicks were hatched – the first recorded successful breeding since 1416. Wilding, or rewilding, therefore represents a fundamental change to the landscape on a scale never attempted in the recent past, but it is proving contentious and divisive in many localities.[18]

In Sussex, many neighbouring farmers were dismayed by the return to nature at Knepp, which overturned generations of farming stewardship, which had enclosed, drained, fertilized and cropped those fields. The idea of handing over land or a farm to the next generation in a 'better' state than they had found it is deeply rooted in the farming world. This also applies to livestock farmers, for whom the herd book charting the history of a flock or cattle herd is as important as the family bible. Abandoning years of endeavour will be understandably resisted. How willing are we to let go and step back?

Hedges in the landscape

The landscape of lowland England after enclosure is defined by rectangular fields bounded by hedges. This aerial photograph, dated from the 1950s prior to the building of the city of Milton Keynes, illustrates the density of hedges at that time. (Photograph from the archive of the Milton Keynes Development Authority)

From wheat to wildlife: thinking big in East Anglia

For many years the proponents of some form of rewilding in Britain have been on the margins of farming. Talk of lynx in the uplands and beavers in the rivers scared off many farmers. Commercial farms concentrated on the main business of increased yields and making a profit. There is now a perceptible change of mood, with more large farming outfits making changes, either to a more nature-friendly way of operating, or a complete swing of turning land over to natural regeneration.

In East Anglia a project known as WildEast has brought together three large farms, which together account for 8,000 acres. The landowners have decided to turn over a fifth of the land to wildlife, and are urging others in the region to follow their lead. This movement seeks to involve other minor landholders, including schools and churches, in an attempt to reverse the decline in biodiversity in a region where large-scale commercial agriculture is the prevalent form of land use.

The enthusiasts for this scheme are clear-sighted. They are aware of the post-Brexit move to public funds for public goods and the premium market for sourcing food, especially high-quality meat. What is different about this initiative is the effort to engage the wider public across East Anglia. 'We have tidied up nature and swept it away in the last 40 years. We have started this scheme to make the conversation public.'[19]

Accidental wildlife

The Common Poppy is one of many weeds of cultivation, controlled in commercial arable crops by herbicide application. The seeds, however, lie dormant for many years and provide a stunning display when arable fields are placed in Countryside Stewardship, as in this illustration from the edge of chalk downland in the eastern Chilterns. (Photograph by Richard Revels)

All of the attempts to encourage a wilder Britain are supported by the Rewilding Britain organization, whose goal is 'Bringing nature back to life'. Many of the efforts hinge on voluntary help, local fundraising and the prospect of some revenue from nature-based tourism. The Wildlife Trusts have set out a pathway to achieving this in a report entitled, *Towards a Wilder Britain*, which explains the importance of public engagement and the use of simple tools – such as mapping the environment – in order to identify areas where people can participate.[20]

Towards a recovering landscape, where nature is normal

A consistent theme of conservation organizations in Britain, such as the Wildlife Trusts, is the plea for a wilder, greener and more diverse Britain. There has always been public acknowledgement that wildlife and wild places are valuable for their own sake and this principle is now accepted as what politician's call, 'in the national interest'. Additionally, there is mounting evidence from across the globe that a healthy, wildlife-rich natural world is essential for our individual well-being and our collective prosperity.

However, every environmental television documentary comes with a warning. In Britain as elsewhere, wildlife is becoming more and more precarious, and this decline has been happening for decades. Wild places are now fewer in number, smaller, more isolated and under threat. In 2010, the Lawton Report reached these same conclusions and went on to issue a blunt warning that the trends and the approach to conservation and protection of wildlife sites were simply not working. There is less nature and green space in the places where we live and work, and not everyone has equal access to nature or to the benefits of being outdoors. In short, nature needs help to recover and this is vital for all of us, as well as the future of wild plants and animals. The lockdown period in early 2020 reinforced this imperative, as many more people, from diverse backgrounds, moved into the countryside in search of exercise, fresh air and as an escape from tedium.

These sentiments are shared by Government and the policy statements accompanying the new Environment Bill are stark, using words not usually found in official pronouncements:

> *Nature is in long-term decline globally and at home. These matters, not only because people care about wildlife in its own right, but because nature ... our ecosystems and their component species ... play a vital role in climate-change mitigation, by removing, trapping and storing carbon, as well as in pollination, flood alleviation, and public health and well-being.* [21]

Another key pronouncement from the same course is even more damming:

Depleted, fragmented, fragile ... we have torn great holes in the web of life that supports us.

The Water Authority and the beavers:
A nature recovery network in action

The key to success in the operation of Nature Recovery Networks is to achieve a strong working relationship between all the partners. The mix of organizations is important in bringing together public bodies, conservation agencies, private landowners, and the volunteers essential for providing on-the-ground support work. Everyone needs to feel there is a gain for their specific interests. In Nottinghamshire, The Severn Trent Water Authority, as a major landowner and funding provider, has built a strong relationship with local Wildlife Trust and tenant farmers, to pioneer a Recovery Network, centred on the River Trent.

The water authority has a clear main goal: to protect the quality of the water supply in the river and manage flooding. Working with the Wildlife Trust, the ambitious plan is to work across 5,000 hectares, with a detailed nature-improvement plan budgeted until 2027. The principle is to bring about improvements which each part of the partnership can celebrate as a success. The restoration of meadows, tree-planting and the creation of ponds are all in the interests of conservation groups, and flood-management is important to local farmers. Ultimately there is an aspiration to introduce beavers at some point, which would guarantee public interest.

To make this real, The Wildlife Trusts across Britain have pioneered the 'Nature Recovery Network' initiative, which brings space for nature into the heart of farming and planning systems and complements the proposed Environment Bill currently under consideration at Westminster. A headline from this initiative is the call for every child to have access to natural places beyond the school nature table. The idea is to encourage communities to work towards a recovering landscape, where nature is *normal* and children grow up with trees to climb, ponds to investigate and fields to explore. The key element is to work towards *greening* communities wherever possible. and in urban areas engaging people in the aim of wilder cities, with green roofs, green walls, pocket parks and city farms. In the wider landscape the trusts use the phrase 'a buzzing countryside', where farmland is criss-crossed by habitats attractive to pollinators. In the uplands, overgrazed grasslands, give way to more trees, restored peat bogs reduce the impact of flooding and the whole landscape act as a store for atmospheric carbon dioxide.

What is inspirational about this initiative is that these networks engage people locally, working literally at ground level, and place communities at the centre of improvements. Networks use maps of local areas to identify sites for improvement and possible new locations for wildlife enhancement, and then move on to target the funding required. This approach has been pioneered on the River Aire, in Yorkshire, where a study of the catchment took the existing agricultural subsidy regime, which paid £263 million over ten years, and modelled how this could be better spent to improve wildlife habitats, without a reduction in farm incomes. The public benefits would, for example, include a reduction in flooding across the lowlands including Leeds. In the Midlands, the River-Trent lowlands have also established an ambitious Nature Recovery Network, with support from a major public body.

At the centre of these Government aspirations is the idea that we should leave the natural world in a better state than we found it. This immediately raises the possibility of trying to make a real and long-lasting impact to restore an environment from a presently degraded to a much-improved level. Is the idea that we should simply *do no more harm* adequate? Or does it lack vision?

Land developers such as house builders have gone some way to incorporate this into planning for future schemes and, following a consultation in 2018, the Department of Food and Rural Affairs (Defra), announced in March 2019 that the concept of 'net biodiversity gain' from any new development would become mandatory. Although this may seem like good news, environmental organizations have urged caution and pointed out that any project intending to improve biodiversity needs to be long term and part of an agreed plan, such as a local Nature Recovery Network. Sites should be connected to adjacent green areas if possible, and simple offsetting designs such as new sports pitches in return for more houses should not be considered as a net biodiversity gain. In contrast, planning green corridors, local nature reserves and tree-planting would all be considered a net gain.

Some environmentalists have embraced this idea on the basis that house-building and other development in the countryside are inevitable and it is therefore better to work *with* the developers; others are cautious – even suspicious – of short-term and ill-thought-out schemes which are of dubious value. The need for a careful survey at the planning stage, as well as consultation with environmental groups are essential, as is the outreach into any new communities to explain the thinking and encourage local involvement from the beginning.

Accidental wildlife

When an environmentalist remarks that, 'the best way to improve wildlife on arable fields is to build houses', there is something strange going on. Ecologists have highlighted the observation that much of commercially farmed arable land with a single crop was not ideal for biodiversity, whereas houses with multiple, variable gardens could provide wildlife pockets of refuge for many common birds and insects. *The Accidental Countryside* by Peter Moss draws attention to the amazing ability of wildlife to colonize the gaps in the human landscape from peregrine falcons on the towers of Norwich cathedral, to urban reservoirs which are a refuge for wintering wildfowl. Sewage works have long been the preferred spot for dedicated birdwatchers.[24] Every county in England has leftover sites at the edge: neither urban or countryside, often an old quarry, a disused railway siding, or a short stretch of former road. These may be brown-field sites and therefore prime candidates for housing. Having no protection, they tend to disappear and the wildlife with them. This is the 'in-between land' at the edges where the urban meets the rural, in the spaces left by previous industry. A 2020 documentary by Helen Macdonald explored the seemingly unpromising land adjacent to the M25 motorway, and revealed a surprising variety of wildlife and biodiversity.[23]

In Bedfordshire, the extensive former brickworks in the clay-rich Marston Vale have been turned successfully into a country park with a protected wildlife site. This attracts wetland species and wildfowl, notably the rare and secretive bittern. This is a deliberate transformation, but many sites are simply abandoned and are then effectively rewilded, often with surprising results. As Peter Moss points out, these places are not really 'bolt-on extras', but part of the web of nature, which has been depleted across the surrounding intensively farmed landscape.[24] When we reflect on the statistic that sparrow populations – historically, the most ubiquitous of urban birds – have declined by 50 per cent plus since 1970, then any unused corners and planned gardens become important refuges for accidental wildlife.

***

Despite surprising *accidental* incursions and marginal gains, such as the return of otters to some streams and rivers, the reported loss of wildlife across Britain remains at a damagingly high level. The inescapable conclusion, mapped out by a series of painstakingly researched reports, is that nature is in trouble, and without determined and sustained action future, generations will inherit a severally depleted environment. There are signals that these messages are now well understood and accepted by the public, and as is often the case, pressed from below by environmental groups and dedicated individuals, this is moving the Government machinery. The Environment and Agricultural Bills will enshrine improved nature protection in law. Added to this are signals that developers, pressured by vocal environmental groups, could take improved biodiversity seriously, by acting on the concept of 'net biodiversity gain', now rebranded as 'net environmental gain'. The established environmental organizations, backed by an army of local volunteers, are well positioned to focus minds on areas where environmental damage is taking place. Local and timely action has achieved some surprising results.

If action in defence of nature is accepted, then choices seem to be opening up. Alternatives include more protected reserves which are well managed, but nature is confined behind a fence, or within restructuring policies which provide funding for the farming sector and encourage more 'nature-friendly' farming in general. The Government proposals for subsidy reform are designed to move farmers towards this second approach.[25]

If, however, the clamour for increased food-security returns, then the competition for land will inevitably squeeze conservation and wildlife back into the margins. In addition, the desire to plant trees on an unprecedented scale has now won political acceptance and there may be an opportunity to direct this planting towards woodlands, which encourage wildlife as well as timber, and avoid the sterile ranks of conifers so heavily criticized in the past. Again, this places further pressure on the land resource.

Restoration of habitats

Conservation management often requires careful intervention to either restore or create a habitat which will provide a home for wildlife. In this photograph the RSPB is working to restore an area of lowland heath threatened by encroaching tree saplings and at the same time ponds are being dug to encourage amphibians.

Climate will have an impact on the efforts in Britain to balance food security, wildlife and the pressing need to store carbon. The weather story of 2019, with widespread flooding followed by unprecedented drought in the spring of 2020, is a reminder that the climate concerns have not gone away. As predicted, weather fluctuations show up in the food chain. Early reports of harvest yields across England in 2020 were pessimistic. Consecutive seasons of extreme weather has seen yields reduced by a third, resulting in the worst harvest outcome since the mid-1980s.[26]

The dilemma is to balance food production with the concerns around environment and a move away from intensive farming. Can food security also allow space for nature-friendly farming to flourish? Can environmental improvement and higher yields be balanced? And can this be achieved as weather patterns change in ways which are difficult to forecast? At the same time, there is the question of how to utilize spare land to keep people there and sustain rural livelihoods. These and other issues will become more pressing as a regime of spending public funds to ensure public goods is implemented from 2021 onwards. Both farmers and the general public interested in the fate of the hedgehog are unsure of the answer.

CHAPTER FOUR

One Degree, Two Degrees, Three Degrees, and More

Emissions must peak in 2020 if we want to limit warming
to 1.5 degrees centigrade as set in the Paris Agreement.

(Christiana Figueres, Chair of the 2015 Paris Accord meeting)[1]

The quote above, from the Costa Rican scientist and diplomat who
helped hammer out the limited agreement during the Paris climate
talks in 2015, sets a clear agenda for the decade. This time marker is
one reason for attempting to draw the issues together in this book.
By early 2020 there was added impetus to break out of the stalemate
surrounding international action on climate, especially in the UK.
Preparations for the 2020 Conference of the Parties' (CoP-26)
international climate meeting, scheduled for Glasgow, had set
ambitious targets to achieve a carbon-neutral economy in the UK by
2050. Proposed Government legislation in Agriculture and
Environment outlined the means by which this could be achieved.

However, since 2015, the willingness of governments to tackle
what is now described as the 'climate emergency' had waned, with
the meeting in Madrid in 2019 only reinforcing the urgency, but not
agreeing any new targets.[2] In early 2020 the publication of a popular
book by Mark Lynes with the stark title, *The Final Warning: Six Degrees
of Climate Emergency*, reinforced the urgency of trying to stick to these

global targets and his assessment of the likely damage which would be caused by even a small rise in global temperatures, added to the fear and anxiety.[3]

Reports from the Madrid gathering underlined the paralysis around the climate issue, by using diplomatic phrases such as 'partial agreement' and the need for more 'ambitious targets'. There was then a hope that the meeting scheduled for late 2020 would re-energize the process. Interestingly, the searingly hot summer in Australia had already set in motion a season of unprecedented fires, which did not seem to make an immediate impact on the Madrid talks. However, the fires gathered pace and spread widely during January 2020. By early February over thirty people had lost their lives, together with many millions of animals in the outback. During February 2020, widespread flooding swept across England and Wales, bringing environmental and climatic issues again into the news. Then came the pandemic, and the climatic question was overtaken by events. The Glasgow Conference was postponed until late 2021.

This global context is the background to the ongoing response to climate change which, at government level in the UK, is led by the Committee for Climate Change (CCC). In November 2018, this powerful government committee added weight to the arguments that land and how it is used needs to become a central part of the thinking in regard to efforts to ameliorate climate change, especially concerning carbon storage. This is a significant shift as agriculture, the primary land user in the UK, then takes on an additional responsibility other than simply the production of food. The countryside has become a carbon store, as well as a food producer. The CCC makes the case that the countryside provides what are now described as 'ecological services', which include the provision of clean water, healthy soils, the protection of wildlife, flood prevention and, of course, food production. A multifunctional landscape is the aspiration.[4] [5]

The estimate is that the farm sector is responsible for around 9 per cent of the UK's greenhouse-gas emissions. In an effort to show that these could be reduced, in 2019 the National Farmers' Union (NFU) responded with bold ideas, setting out what was feasible by adopting a target of *a net carbon- zero agricultural* sector by 2040 – a decade ahead of the overall government target.[6] The most important aspect of the plan was to refine the way in which land was used on UK farms, in order to capture more carbon from the atmosphere and then retain carbon in the form of organic matter in the soils. In practical terms this requires more and bigger hedgerows, increased on-farm tree-planting, attention paid to increased carbon stored in the top soil of arable land, and perhaps more land in grassland and pasture. In all, an environment-friendly approach to agriculture. All these measures would herald a significant change in the countryside's appearance and benefit wildlife immensely.

Over the past decade farmers have faced criticism especially over greenhouse-gas emissions from the livestock industry, which at the same time is dealing with the trend away from meat and dairy towards a plant-based diet. This issue of declining meat consumption shows an interesting divide between those who predict that this will continue, with fewer grazing animals overall, concentred on more intensive farms and, unsurprisingly, the opposite NFU view – a landscape with more animals, not fewer, producing premium-quality meat. An ambitious target of a carbon-zero farm sector by 2040 will place grazed pasture, and therefore meat, at the centre of the plan. The argument centred on carbon storage and the impact on climate then begins to include issues of animal welfare, the environmental impact of intensive animal production, the stocking rates of sheep, especially on marginal hill land, and future imports of meat and chicken. These all impact on the profitability of farm enterprises, and so a single issue around climate becomes more complex.

***

The reforms promised in the forthcoming Agriculture and Environmental Bills are all geared towards achieving radical change. Steps to encourage tree-planting and peatland restoration, for example, will make significant differences and impact on the countryside we are familiar with. The consensus is that farming will need to cope with increased risks from more extreme weather events, including dry summers, with consequently longer droughts, and probable increased winter rainfall. The winter of 2019/20 and the following spring and early summer provided an example of what growing conditions might look like in the future. A very wet winter curtailed the drilling of winter wheat across Britain, forcing many arable farms to gamble on better conditions in the spring. This did arrive, but late, forcing spring-sown crops to also be drilled late. This was then followed by extremely dry conditions into June. Letters to *The Times* in late May used words like 'drought'. The old farm saying that yields were '10 per cent land-management and 90 per cent luck with the weather' was again proving true. My mid-2020 the impact on yields was felt as harvesting began, with wheat yields reduced by a third, and the estimated total harvest falling to levels not recorded since the 1980s.[7]

Some farms with access to capital are already moving to high-technology solutions to stabilize yield. The expansion of irrigated crops, usually reserved for high-value horticultural production, is being more widely considered which places more demand on falling water levels in aquifers, especially in the chalk areas of southern England. Permanent drought conditions have been forecast for southern England by 2045.[8] More attention is being paid to operations in the field, including the careful measurement of fertilizer and pesticide application, sowing seed as efficiently as possible and measuring yield direct from the combine harvester. This level of precision farming is already well advanced across the bigger farms of England and Wales. All of these precision measures demand investment, efficient farms and bigger field sizes, which allow the appropriate machinery. This is the intensification of agriculture often serviced by borrowing, which results in the following questions:

- Can this approach be married with appropriate environmental changes?

- Does this level of intensive production allow for wildlife-friendly farming?

- Can this be combined with retaining hedgerows, on-farm tree-planting, wider field margins, and a reduced number of animals on the uplands?

- Can these approaches be brought together in a subsidy framework and how can the funds be monitored?

- How do we measure success? And

- If the subsidy fails to make a difference, is there a willingness to change direction?

All of the above make prediction difficulty and add to the uncertainty for the farming community.

The difficulty is attempting to assess the specific impacts of the likely climate scenarios and across what time scale, in order to know which is most harmful and how these will all play out across the landscape. Natural England has made a stab at this with impact assessments within selected parts of the country. The research study for Sherwood Forest, for example, noted that: dry summers would place many trees under stress, risking attack from the increasing numbers of tree diseases; commercial agriculture, which depended on high-value crops, would require more irrigation from groundwater; and extreme rainfall could place bare soils at risk from serious erosion in the springtime.[9] For instance, a farm growing a high-value crop such as asparagus or early potatoes, where the soil can be exposed in spring, would face soil being potentially washed off the field during heavy rain storms.

More generally, as all UK natural ecosystems are shaped by the weather, they will be sensitive to any significant climate change. There is now a well-established upward curve in average temperatures over the past forty years which has had an impact on wildlife. There is agreement that since the 1970s there has been a one-degree centigrade rise in average temperatures. Although this seems small, the implication is that this will continue unless emissions are cut quickly and sharply. New species are arriving in Britain from mainland Europe and, within Britain, distributions are shifting to the north, making an adjustment necessary to what ecologists call their 'climate space'; that is, the climatic range within which they will thrive. Although some groups of insects will see this 'climate space' expand, larger species such as birds and most plants are likely to enjoy less expansion.

In a series of detailed research studies, the UK Climatic Change Risk Assessment, makes the point that, in theory, a warming climate should make British wildlife richer and more diverse, but this will only happen if there are suitable habitats to expand into. This requires an adequately sized habitat already in a good ecological condition. If the woodlands, heath and hedgerows are in poor condition, then a warmer climate will not make any beneficial expansion. Heathland is a particularly stark example of this, as at the national level the remaining patches of heathland are often isolated. Recent work on heathland sites in Bedfordshire is, therefore, strategically important as a link between areas south of the Thames and the Suffolk coast. However, heathland is particularly vulnerable to fire, which poses an additional threat.

Overall, the condition of the habitat is the key factor. The most significant adverse impact of climate change is probably on peat bogs, mires and fens, which have suffered severe ecological decline: some 70 per cent of the deep peats in England are presently degraded due to overgrazing, rotational burning and excessive drainage. Any acceleration towards further drying, and therefore a greater risk of fire in these environments, could be a tipping point. The problem in these wetland environments is undoubtedly climatic, owing to the further release of carbon, combined with the loss of a unique habitat.

Although it is imperative to concentrate on the direct and immediate threats, there will be unavoidable, less obvious risks. On the landscape scale there are likely to be changes across significant areas which will influence how we view the countryside overall. Much-loved landscapes may alter over a lifetime. One indirect outcome is the threat to what are now referred to as 'cultural landscapes', such as the Lake District National Park or the landscape of the Orkney islands. Along the coastline of eastern England, the impacts are already clear.[10]

Rescued from the sea

The coast of northeast England is experiencing significant erosion from rising sea levels and storm surges in the North Sea. Sea erosion has revealed important archaeological finds. Occasional finds of Bronze Age and older artefacts at a site at Low Hauxley, south of Amble, Northumberland led to excavations in 1983, 2008 and again in 2014. Excavation exposed buried soil horizons and peat layers below the sand dune cover. These allowed archaeologists to build a picture of settlement from the very early Mesolithic (around 10,000 BP) to an important Bronze age cemetery (around 4,000 BP) containing pottery and cremated burial remains. Top picture- the site protected from the sea during excavation. Lower picture- a reconstructed bronze age urn from the Low Hauxley site. (pictures from Archaeological Research Services Ltd).

Rescue what you can: King Canute and the archaeologists

In 2009 a dog walker on the beach at Druridge Bay, on the Northumberland Coast, noticed an unusual layer of materials in the exposed sandy deposits of the cliff face, which had been recently eroded by a storm. As these beaches are at risk from storm surges related to sea-level rise, new exposures in the sand dunes flanking the beach are common and this walker had enough knowledge to call in professional archaeological advice. A rapid inspection determined this was an important site and a full excavation was mounted by Archaeological Research Services, which ultimately uncovered a Bronze-Age cemetery, complete with cremation burials and well-preserved pottery.[11]

These Northumberland beaches, in common with many coastal locations along the east coast of Britain, are at imminent risk of erosion. Although the most obvious concerns are the risk to property, the loss of agricultural land and the imminent flooding of communities, there is also a slow erosion of what have been called 'cultural landscapes'. This threat is especially urgent, as climate change gathers pace and sea levels rise. Estimates of sea-level rise are usually given in a range of values which vary, depending on factors such as the amount of future greenhouse-gas emissions, and the forecast increase in severe winter storm events in the North Sea. A storm surge will magnify any gradual rise in sea level on this coast. A further complication is the slow but steady sinking of the land in eastern and southern England, related to its geology. The best estimates centre around a 40 cm rise by 2050 and 80 cm by the end of the century.[12] Sites at risk include the Saxon Shore Roman defensive works, dating from the third century AD, along the coast from Suffolk to the Isle of Wight.

***

The difficulty predicting climate warming is working out specific impacts, especially across a varied landscape and setting out a possible timeline. There is no dispute that climate changes are underway – a 'known unknown' – but how exactly to prepare for the changed circumstances is still unclear. Prudent and pragmatic responses include the storage of carbon in soils, peatlands, trees and grass pasture. However, the aspiration for a carbon-neutral economy by 2050 will depend on such actions working on a large scale. This makes the role of Government important in using policy actions to ensure that public funds are employed in the public interest. The proposed adjustments to funding support through farm subsidy offer such an opportunity, but implementing this in a fair way which achieves a measurable outcome will be difficult.

At the same time, it is understood that not all changes will be harmful. The expansion northwards of English wine production is one example, with new vineyards being planted in locations which mirror the distribution of monastic viticulture in the twelfth and thirteenth centuries. The Royal Horticultural Society (RHS) has even added a page of advice to its website for ambitious viticulturalists.

In summary, although there will be some gains to the environment, the impact of rising temperature is expected to make the existing problems around degraded and fragile habitats worse – in some cases, such as upland peat, it is likely to be much worse. David Thompson, a US-based climate scientist, explained the dilemma.

> The UK's rich wildlife and distinctive landscapes are a source of inspiration to millions of people. Many believe that society has a 'moral duty' to protect nature for current and future generations. There is also a growing recognition that 'natural capital' – our water, soils, land, sea, air and the wildlife they sustain – is as important for people's well-being and quality of life as economic and social capital.[13]

The words which spring out of this quote are 'moral duty', which echoes the moral stance set out by Government that this generation should be the first to leave behind an improved environment. This is close to the ethic of many farmers, managing land with a sense of stewardship and handing on a farm in a better state. It may mean hard choices nationally, and ultimately will involve funding and selecting priorities. What is emerging is the understanding that the warming climate will certainly bring changes, only some of which can be managed. The damaging effects will be most severe where nature is already struggling, habitats are degraded and wildlife is confined to fragile reserves and small pockets of land.

What is now clear is that a more resilient natural environment, managed and better connected at both local and national levels, can no longer be considered an afterthought. 'Resilience' has become a much-used term meaning the ability to cope with changes both known and unknown. This will require that nature be considered part of the fabric of society, not just as an extra and separate from mainstream economic life.

One of the most visible and disturbing signals accompanying climate change is an increase in extreme events, usually flooding, which is now more widespread and increasingly common across the UK. In coastal areas, a measurable rise in sea levels is already leading to land being surrendered to the sea. In the next chapter we explore if the choice is to build bigger defences in urban areas or make changes to the land use in the uplands to slow and reduce floods. Our choices will be determined by what we expect from the countryside. Are we willing to engage in working out the value of these areas and the mounting costs of defence as the climate warms?

CHAPTER FIVE

Taming the Flood

HOTSPUR: And here the smug and silver Trent shall run

In a new channel, fair and evenly;

It shall not wind with such a deep intent

To rob me of so rich a bottom here.

GLENDOWER: Not wind! It shall, you see it doth.

(Henry IV, Part I: III, i)

The epigraph above illustrates the historic struggle to prevent flooding along major rivers, which defeated Hotspur and many others since.[1] This book was written during 2020, but by February the Atlantic winter storms had begun to press in from the west and dump heavy rainfall across areas as far apart as South Wales, Cumbria and Yorkshire. Storm Ciara was followed within days by Storm Dennis, with rain lashing across a wide area of Britain, adding yet more water to already saturated ground.[2] The amounts of rain were often described as 'unprecedented' and both flooding levels and meteorological records began to be swept away like vehicles in the path of the rivers taking over urban streets. By 16 February there were 346 flood alerts across England and Wales, including 4 at the level that warned of 'potential loss of life'. February 2020 was the wettest month since records began in 1910. In late March, when the country was gripped by a public health emergency, parts of Herefordshire remained under water, and five warnings remained in place until early May.

The media coverage in 2020 followed a well-worn pattern familiar from previous flood events in Carlisle, York, Tewkesbury and Morpeth. Stories appeared of individuals with lives turned upside down mixed with stories of the family dog rescued from the flood. This was then followed by a search for someone to blame, bringing direct fire to bear on the Environment Agency, local government and, ultimately, national politicians. Spokespersons then appeared armed with statistics. In early 2020, £2.6 billion were already being spent and additional commitments costing £4 billion were made quickly to strengthen flood defences. Engineering calculations are beginning to reflect this urgency, in light of a rethinking of the previous assumption that there would be a major flood once in 100 years. In the face of future unpredictable events in different locations, the Met Office is promising faster and more localized forecasting with greater precision in the future thanks to the purchase of a new supercomputer at a cost of £1.2 billion. The overall funding promises require serious budget pledges.

Occasionally there is a slot in the news-reporting of flooding events which looks behind the immediate story and asks fundamental questions, such as: Are floods becoming more common? Is flooded Britain a 'new normal'?[3] There is now an acceptance that the scale and speed of the flooding is increasing, and it is becoming more widespread. Reports often reflect this with flood victims commenting:

'In the past this was a once-in-a-generation' occurrence. Now it is happening every second year'; or, 'This flood is much higher than in the past'; Records bear this out with the record height in Hereford, set in 1794, exceeded in mid-February 2020; by the end of March some 5,000 homes had been flooded.[4]

In the UK we may have been slow to grasp the reality of more frequent and more intense rainfall periods, as they are masked by the *normal* unpredictable weather patterns across these islands. In other parts of the world, with more stable weather patterns, the rise in global temperature due to climatic warming is easier to plot. However, when it comes to rainfall, the records show that large parts of the UK are now experiencing exceptional deluges outside the scope of historical patterns. Estimates of the value of properties at risk in England, prepared a decade ago, gave a figure of £5.2 million. Are these figures still relevant in the quickening climatic changes now underway? The cost of flooding in 2009 was thought to be close to £1 billion every year but is now estimated at twice this figure.[5]

Such large numbers are difficult to relate to, and a statistic which may more impact is a forecast that 23 of the 92 football league stadiums in England can expect partial or total flooding in the next 30 years. Supporters of Carlisle United will have no difficulty understanding this, with flooding in 2005, 2015, and in a less damaging way in 2017.

Since the traumatic events when Storm Desmond brought chaos to Cumbria, especially in Carlisle and Kendal in 2015, there have been constant calls to look at the catchments of the flood-prone rivers and attempts, to set in place a process to slow the flow of the streams in the upper valleys. The phrase 'flattening the curve', familiar from the Covid-19 pandemic, is the same principle: buy time in front of the flood and reduce the immediate flood peak. This approach is sometimes referred to as 'soft engineering' and is contrasts the engineering solutions which move water away faster and which may imperil communities downstream. It remains to be seen if the cycle of flood, build a defence, flood again, and build even higher will ever be enough to cope with the climatic changes now underway.

The title of this chapter, 'Taming the Flood' is borrowed from a book and television series in the late 1980s, in which Jeremy Purseglove argued for a new approach to wetlands and rivers.[6] He argued that engineers were concerned mostly with moving river water from A to B as fast as possible, which underrated the importance of wetlands and rivers in all land-based ecosystems. Since this publication (reissued in 2015), a more sensitive approach has gained ground especially in Europe, where engineers and land managers frequently use descriptions such as 'making room for the river', and 'giving back land to the river', when planning flood-prevention works.

In the uplands of western and northern Britain, much of the river-catchment land is covered by hill peat – or it was! Drainage for upland grazing and burning for grouse-shooting have degraded this sponge-like peat, allowing water to reach the streams, and ultimately, the flooding rivers, much more quickly. The burning of heather to encourage young shoots and provide a mix of habitats for grouse has long been criticized for encouraging gullying and adding to the flood hazard. When mature vegetation is encouraged without burning, and peat bogs are restored, water is held on the moor for longer. Plant cover and peat both slow the flood. The Government had begun to recognize the problem and was meant to be encouraging a voluntary reduction in peat-burning. There was also the promise that this would be banned eventually. Presently an English peat strategy launched in August 2019 is still pending.[7] Meanwhile villages such as Hebden Bridge, snug in the valley below moorland, continue to flood.[8]

Likewise, the events in Cumbria in 2015 prompted a discussion on tree cover in the landscape and the capacity of woodlands to reduce the peaks of large floods. A substantial scientific review of the existing knowledge by the Centre for Ecology and Hydrology reached a mixed conclusion, that:

> Considering all statements together, distinguishing only on the basis of increasing or decreasing cover, there is broad support for the conclusion that trees influence flood peaks. Increasing the amount of tree cover results in a decreasing flood peak, and decreasing the amount of tree cover results in an increase in the flood peak.[9]

However, the findings were not as clear-cut as they might seem: the positive impact on small floods was agreed, but with a large flood the role of tree cover appears less effective. The dense stocking of sheep on the Cumbrian fells is a similar catchment problem, which was given serious attention after the 2015 floods. These flocks are, at best, marginally profitable, requiring subsidies to enable these hill farms to continue. If flooding is to be reduced downstream there may need to be some reduction in sheep numbers to allow space for different types of land use, including trees. At this point there are difficult questions around farm livelihoods and what we expect from a National Park. In a similar way there are serious questions about moor burning for shooting. Rural livelihoods are at risk and the landscape appearance would need to alter significantly to provide a measure of flood protection downstream.

The experience in Kendal in Cumbria illustrates the problem, where the people of the town are faced with a high flood-defence wall which will cut through the heart of the community and also require the felling of many urban trees. This has sparked a debate on the choices available.

On the lowlands the unprecedented level of planning applications, estimated at over a quarter of a million pounds, for new homes on the existing Green Belt further reduces the capacity of land to absorb sudden downpours. Hard surfaces of any development, including house roofs and hard tarmac infrastructure, decants water quickly into drains, streams and eventually flooded rivers. The benefit of the new homes is reduced if other properties are flooded downstream.

One of the predictable outcomes of any flood event is that there are alarm calls over the building of new homes on river flood plains. This, like many problems associated with the environment, is complicated as there are a number of opposing forces pulling in different directions, one of which is the pressing demands for homes. Add climate change with more frequent severe storms, increased winter rainfall and water being passed quickly into drains and rivers from hard surfaces, and flood plains are more likely to be under water. That is why they are called 'flood' plains. Nevertheless, there is curiously a deep-rooted human desire to live in proximity to water.

Rivers verses drains

When urban areas flood the damage to homes and business is immediately obvious. However, flooding of agricultural land also leads to substantial losses of crops and livestock, as well as damage to farm land and property. Agricultural land can be used to hold back and temporarily store floodwaters avoiding more expensive urban flooding and there is a strong case to pay farmers for this 'flood risk management service'. (Flooding of farm land in the River Tone, Somerset, Winter 2013/14 from Joe Morris.)

Kendal:

stopping the flood, but dividing the town

Kendal, a town of 28,500 people, was one of many in the north-west of England swamped yet again by the February 2020 floods. As the townspeople explained wearily, they had been here before when Storm Desmond hit in December 2015 and flooded over 2,275 properties in the town. Following that event, a flood plan was designed at the eye-watering cost of £76 million, mostly from EU funding, which combined both the improvement of the immediate town defences and work in the catchments of the rivers flowing into the River Kent, and onwards through the town.

Although the need for expensive physical flood defences was accepted, the social cost of implementing that these works would have on a popular tourist town was also considered to be high. The plan would require the felling of at least 500 trees across the town, and alarmingly, the building of 6 kilometres of 2-metre-high concrete walls, described by locals as, 'the wall which will divide the town'. To make these barriers more tolerable, Perspex windows would be added to reduce the impact of the concrete barriers.

In addition, there would be some funds for improving natural protection in the uplands by creating storage areas at a cost of around £800,000. These techniques, described as 'natural flood-management', have had some success elsewhere. Slowing the flood waters by using restored peat cover, digging ponds and other small storage areas in the valley bottoms, and planting trees are accepted as beneficial. The problem is that these are abstract ideas and it's difficult to measure their exact impact on a flood. In contrast, a wall is visible and flood peaks are easy to monitor. Engineers know these interventions work, but by how much and exactly where is uncertain. Local governments, sensitive to criticism, are always more likely to build upwards. In Europe the experience has been that a wall of dykes eventually encourages increased development behind the defence, which is a risky option. This is known as the 'dyke paradox' in the Netherlands.[10]

Desirable property with a river view, or part of a flood ghetto?

When the village of Fishlake in South Yorkshire was under water and evacuated in November 2019, a search of estate agents' properties on offer throughout Britain showed multiple properties close to a river. Houses with river frontage, close to a marina or a bankside pub, all commanded a premium price. The closeness to water is a unique selling point on the property market. Think of how many pubs there are with names such as the Ferryman, the Boat Inn, or the Swan. One of the consistent themes following any flooding event are calls for more control on building new homes on flood plains. What is going on here? Developers are attracted to sites close to water, planners are concerned, the insurance industry asks for higher premiums or refuses to insure ... and yet houses are in demand. There seem to be a number of conflicting issues at work.

Firstly, the pressure to build new homes is growing each year. One result is around 200,000 new houses have been built on flood-plain sites in the decade beginning 2001. New building is necessary to reduce the backlog and also meet demand. The most thoughtful examination of the requirement for new homes is a briefing paper from the House of Commons Library, which noted that overall, 345,000 new homes are needed every year in England alone. In the last reported year of 2018/19 some 240,000 were built; a significant shortfall in the requirement.[11] For each development of greater than ten homes, flood-risk advice is required from the Environment Agency. However, the planning authority has the final say. The pressure on each local government to meet housing targets is immense and land on a flood plain is attractive to developers, as it is flat, usually close to infrastructure and often not on prime agricultural land. Developers often argue that, with investment, these homes can be protected from any present flood danger, but future flooding may not be so easy to control on vulnerable sites.

Secondly, flood protection is expensive. In the March 2020 budget the Chancellor, doubled the spending on protection to £5.2 billion. Every flooding event leads to increased spending and funds sucked into hard engineering schemes.

Thirdly, there is the inevitability that climate change will increase flood events, with a combination of extreme rainfall and a long-term increase in winter rainfall. When and where these floods will occur can only be guessed at, which new technology, such as the Met Office supercomputer, may eventually assist with. Building more and higher defences cuts off access to the river, such as in Kendal, and ultimately diminishes the assets which it is designed to protect.

The alternative to this hard engineering approach is a combination of 'soft engineering' in the river-catchment, flood meadows, trees on the upper slopes to slow the flood, and deep peat restored across the moorlands. These interventions demand radical thinking as advocated by the Institute and Faculty of Actuaries in 2016.

Government should create a workable, proactive, long-term strategy for dealing with flood risk. This means dealing with the root causes of flooding. A strategy needs to be implemented that recognises the changing nature of flooding and the impact of more frequent and extreme weather.[12]

There are already successful examples of the implementation of holistic natural flood-management when applied along the length of a river course. The town of Pickering, which suffered two episodes of serious flooding in 1999/2000, opted subsequently for changes in the valley upstream of the town, rather than a stark concrete wall. The river course was enhanced through a range of measures, including woody debris dams and flood ponds, which physically hold back the water and slow the flow. Pickering has escaped serious flooding ever since.[13]

Engineered flood barriers will always be an essential element of any protection, but it is becoming clear that flooding cannot be eliminated entirely without attention to the scale of new building on vulnerable sites and imaginative land-use changes in the river catchment. During the flooding in February the Environment Secretary George Eustice admitted that, *'We will never be able to protect every single household'.*[14]

A managed retreat

The same argument applies to coastal flooding, which is now a way of life along stretches of the eastern coastline. Sad photographs of houses perched on the edge of crumbling clay cliffs are a reminder that many of the sea defences were erected following the 1953 floods, which killed over 300 people. With a forecast sea-level rise of around 1.2 metres during this century, combined with more violent North Sea storms, simply building ever-higher defences is too expensive to be a viable option. Faced with the figure of 8,000 homes and businesses which could be lost in England and Wales in the next 20 years, it is time for a different and more radical approach.14 An alternative is to implement a 'managed retreat', with land lost to the sea and replaced over time with a salt-marsh habitat. Research has shown that an 80-metre-wide buffer of marsh could reduce the height of the waves to mere ripples inland.[15]

The National Trust and conservation charities which own sections of this coast have taken up this idea with enthusiasm, expanding salt marches and bringing benefits to bird life and, indirectly, to tourism. At the same time, valued infrastructure and farmland inland has been protected. Any coastal environment will adapt to a rise in sea level by retreating and replacing the shoreline or sea-erodible cliffs with wetland, mudflats or sand dunes, which are all important natural ecosystems. But these natural coastal-protection mechanisms are being squeezed between a rising sea and advancing development, often driven by the desire for a sea view. In many parts of the east coast of England the message is, 'Do not resuscitate'.

***

The questions of river and coastal flooding lead to that of an ecological balance and the social issue of farming and land-management in the uplands and along vulnerable coastlines. The language has changed from 'flood prevention' to 'flood resilience' and, in more technical discussions, the term 'ecological services' is used to describe habitats which increase this resilience to floods. The next step is to attach some values to these ecological services and set them against the cost of reduced flooding downstream, or along a receding coast.

The expectation is that we can call on economists to help make these hard choices. If values are assigned to habitats then decisions are guided by some reality and firm numbers, at least in terms of the costs and benefits. Some of these judgements are simpler to tease out than others. In the example of land lost to the sea, calculations include the income from the land lost for grazing each year set against the gains projected to add to the economy, from tourists and birdwatchers on a salt marsh if the sea is allowed to flood coastal meadows. Economists would regard this example as oversimplistic as it ignores the values attached to nature itself, such as an increase in migratory wildfowl or the biodiversity of the resulting marshland. Placing values on these habitats lifts the argument out of economics into personal experience and choice.

Economists approach these questions using a technique which they have termed 'natural capital accounting', which attempts to estimate these valuations of the natural world by attaching notional costs and values to various landscapes and habitats. Sceptics would question if this is a science or perhaps an art form. Nevertheless, the

Government has now accepted this as the way forward and all major infrastructure work is now subject to this form of analysis.

In the Government review of nature reserves and the state of conservation in England, Professor John Lawton made the point that many parts of society which seem distant from nature and the environment are, on closer inspection, impacted directly.[16] As an example he quotes flooding in urban areas which, with some radical thinking, can be reduced by the creation or re-establishment of wetlands which had been drained previously. This can be a 'win–win' situation. By refining the way in which we value each habitat and estimating the ecological services that nature can provide, the overall benefits to society become both quantifiable and realistic.

These decisions can be very local, such as allowing a few square kilometres of salt marsh to grow as a coastal defence; or national, such as the impact of a livestock subsidy on uplands, which would reduce overall sheep numbers. The coastal retreat at the expense of some buildings and grazing land could provide a buffer to erosion that concrete walls, erected at great expense, may never achieve. On a national scale, the adjustment of subsidies would potentially impact a whole landscape and challenges our notions of what to expect from the countryside, and how we look after what are now referred to as 'cultural landscapes'. Can these also be subjected to the economist's spreadsheet?

Therefore, we arrive back at the opening dilemma: How to place a value on a peat bog or, as posed at the beginning of this book, a skylark. In more pragmatic and human terms, this problem is how to estimate the value of a way of life, such as shepherding Herdwick sheep in a National Park or a clifftop caravan-park business providing enjoyment for families along the coast.

But how much is it worth?

The title of this book is deliberately provocative: it invites the reader to place a value on a skylark, which at first asking seems a ridiculous question. How can one value a bird, even a species, which has inspired poetry and iconic passages of music? Many people kick against the idea of attaching a value to any element of nature, whereas others accept that a rational economic approach may have some merit. Attempting to calculate the cost of losing a wood or river meadows, perhaps forever, provides an argument to think of the environment in different way. The wider picture of valuation becomes clearer when the overall value of a wood can be set against the slowing of a flood event, or the protection of a rare species of plant. Or perhaps a much more difficult calculation: the value placed by people who use the wood for exercise or spiritual renewal. The calculations then move well beyond orthodox economics.

This approach of attempting to calculate and attach value to any landscape habitat is relatively new and has introduced into the language a bundle of new terms such as 'natural capital'. A useful definition is taken from the 2018 Government's, *25-Year Environment Plan*, which defined natural capital as:

... the sum of our ecosystems species, fresh-water, land, soils, minerals, our air and our seas. These are all elements of nature that either directly or indirectly bring value to people and the country at large.[17]

The key part of this quote is calculating, or at least *estimating*, a 'value of natural habitats to people and the country at large'. Think then of the value of a wood. There is a direct benefit to the country overall by providing some degree of flood protection. Flooded homes cost money, and more engineering works cost a lot of money. Additionally, an indirectly value to individuals could be grouped as mental health or well-being, or simply feeling better. These indirect benefits are more problematic to value.

These values are usually described as 'ecosystem services', which describe the part played by the environment and the products of nature, which provide benefits to us all. Examples of this would be such important services as the pollination of crops, clean air and water, healthy soils, timber production, recreational opportunities and overall well-being. Some of these services can be valued, or at least estimated, and some can be guessed at as a cost saved. This is where detractors of the *economics-first* approach label these valuations as absurd. They argue that a healthy soil, for example, is an obvious benefit understood by all, and attempting to calculate a cost associated with any degradation of the topsoil is built on flimsy assumptions. This, they would argue, replaces common sense with economics.[18]

In the same way it may be timely to address some of the misunderstandings which are prevalent regarding the pressures on land in general. If we are to make adjustments to how we use the landscape to prevent flooding and provide other services to the people, then is there land to spare? Don't we live on a crowded island?

A crowded island?

How much of Britain can we spare for wildlife or flood protection or nature conservation? Or to look at this matter differently: How much of the UK is presently built over and considered to be *urban*? Often in discussions over the loss of green-field land to development, the arguments are that, especially in England, the countryside is being 'concreted over'. This is often an emotive issue. Ask an audience to estimate how much land is urban and the range of answers is from 15 to 50 per cent.

It is now possible to be reasonably precise using studies by the UK National Ecosystem Assessment (NEA), which reported a surprising answer in 2014. Land in the UK classified as urban was only 6.8 per cent as the average value. There were regional variations: 10.6 in England; and unsurprisingly, a mere 1.9 per cent in Scotland; with Wales at 4.1 per cent. Therefore, in England, for example, there is around 89 per cent of countryside out there – or there was in 2014![19]

BBC journalist Mark Easton analysed these figures and pointed out that, within the land classed as urban, there are 'green spaces', such as parks, sports grounds and allotments. In fact, such green space was just under half of the land within the urban description and was not built on. Add domestic gardens to these and the area actually built on falls to below 3 per cent. Setting aside quibbles such as the increasing tendency for gardens to be paved over, the headline outcome is that only a small part of England is actually built on and, most importantly, the mental picture which we carry of a crowded and a concreted-over landscape is out of tune with reality. This picture of urban sprawl is something that 80 per cent of people who live in a town carry with them when driving along roads to the next town, or to the next area of built-up Britain. In fact, the countryside is still extensive. There remain many open spaces and we need to decide how we agree to manage them in future. And, of course, we should try to ensure we do not lose more vital green space within the towns and cities, or on a personal level, try to manage gardens in a wildlife-friendly way. Although the landscape we usually see may be built-up and urban, the countryside beyond is still there and now fulfils a whole range of services including water-flow regulation.[20]

Squeezing more from the geological sponge

Paradoxically, although flooding events have caused havoc in northern and western Britain, the chalk landscapes of the English home counties have suffered a very different environmental crisis, with falling water levels in the underlying geology. The result is that small chalk streams, beloved of anglers and entomologists, have dried up or suffered from markedly reduced stream flow. This impacts not only on the aquatic life in the stream, but also the waterside meadows, watercress beds and the chances of seeing the flash of a kingfisher – all are diminished. In many areas the water levels are at the lowest since records began, making this a global concern since England has around three-quarters of the world's chalk streams. This means an increased global responsibility,

Water supply in this region of southern England and into East Anglia relies on the chalk rock and on water extraction from an aquifer which is not being topped up adequately by rainfall to recharge. Only around 15 per cent of rivers in this area could be reported as being in good health. The causes of this decline are evident. This is the area of Britain where the population has been growing, forcing water demand upwards. Rainfall is often concentrated during intense storm events, with water running off rather than moving downwards into the soil and the aquifer. Summers are becoming hotter, hence increasing water demand, and we are all using more water per person. The water consumption in the UK per person is around 140 litres per day, much higher than in other parts of Europe. The use of water for irrigation is important, with economists arguing that water prices are low and farmers and domestic consumers are reluctant to face larger bills. More on-farm reservoirs are one answer, but these eat up useful land and are expensive capital works.

The pressure on water resources, especially in the east and south of England, adds to the perception of a countryside which is crowded. This is further reinforced by living in towns and cities, with occasional visits to the countryside usually revolving around a specific visitor attraction marketed as a 'heritage experience'. The risk here is selling an image to the urban population of the countryside as a string of individual sites – a castle; a stately home; a woodland walk; or a well-known viewpoint – without any understanding of the landscapes inside which these are set.

Efforts to reduce flooding in the lowlands will all add to the complex countryside mosaic. The job description for the countryside is expanding, with flood amelioration added to food production, the storage of carbon, the protection of wildlife and maintaining rural livelihoods. All compete for countryside space. These often-conflicting demands are likely to alter the appearance of an area such as a National Park. This then prompts questions and decisions on what we want and expect from the countryside as the pace of change quickens.

This returns us to the widening expectations now being placed on the landscape. The importance of habitats such as coastal marshes, upland moorland and chalk streams have been sketched to illustrate how these are now understood as critical defences as the climate changes. Building resilience in the land means looking after these habitats, and trying to estimate their overall value. Although setting such economic values may seem an affront to some – how to value a skylark – the reality is that making these judgements may offer the best long-term outcomes for conservation.

In the following chapters we look at the whole landscape rather than individual sites and try to tease out the issues as policy, climate, and how public attitudes change over time.

CHAPTER SIX

Heritage and Cultural Landscapes

Ampthill Park straddles the Greensand Ridge at approximately the midpoint of the long-distance footpath known as the Greensand Ridge Walk, which crosses Bedfordshire from the north-east to the south-west. Local dog walkers in the park far outnumber the long-distance hikers and both enjoy being in a pleasant example of the English parkland countryside, which also offers rewarding views over the Bedfordshire clay plain to the north and east. Few of the walkers realize how amazing these 70 ha of land are as a real-estate bargain. The parkland was purchased by Ampthill Town Council just after the Second World War for the knock-down price of £10,700. To an economist this provides an excellent example of 'public funds' used to secure 'public goods', which means a slice of history is now conserved and managed by a public body at a modest cost to the people of Ampthill. In 2016 grant-funding was obtained from the Heritage Lottery Fund (HLF), which allowed the town council to upgrade facilities and increase access for the less mobile. At the same time there was the opportunity to refresh the information boards and enhance public engagement in various ways.

The Park is a Grade-II-listed area within the Parks and Gardens Schedule maintained by Historic England. This mostly reflects the importance of this parkland as a fine example of the work of Capability

Brown, who was contracted by Lord Ossory in the late eighteenth century to design a landscape which was then fashionable. Ampthill Park incorporates many of Brown's classic signature features such as tree clumps, water features, tree-lined avenues and views of the grand house, all in a very compact area. Access is free! Following the injection of funds from the HLF and celebrations of the tricentenary of the birth of Brown, the town council began to use the term 'Ampthill Great Park' to reflect its earlier history, including the use of this park as a Tudor hunting reserve in the time of Henry VIII. The king did hunt in this vicinity and Catherine of Aragon was imprisoned in Ampthill Castle (no longer standing) before her divorce hearing at Dunstable and subsequent death at Kimbolton Castle. This small fragment of history is marked by street names in the town and an annual festival. Other historical connections are the use of the park by Bedfordshire regiments prior to deployment to the Western Front in the First World War and as a prisoner-of-war camp in the Second World War.

This compact parkland can rightly be described as a 'cultural landscape' spanning a time period from Mesolithic hunter-gatherers, whose flints have been recovered on the edge of the park, to the burial of a model golden hare as an enticement for literary treasure hunters in the late twentieth century. Landscapes such as these are now receiving increased attention and protection as sites with a special heritage value, at both national and international levels.

Presently thirty-one areas in England have been recognized by UNESCO as World Heritage Sites and are included in the UK system with legal protection.[1] These include areas described as 'cultural', such as Kew Gardens and Neolithic Orkney, plus a few locations designated on landscape values alone, such as the Giant's Causeway in Northern Ireland. Such a framework requires the protection of landscapes for the enjoyment of future generations and describes such terrestrial landforms as 'a treasure trove' of both visible and hidden clues about the past.

The Heritage Lottery Fund (now the National Heritage Lottery Fund) also recognizes landscape as a part of the national heritage and identity. An ambitious initiative of Landscape Partnerships was launched to protect and enhance the environment in forty-six areas throughout the UK. The strength of this approach was the broad scope of this endeavour, which has brought together a range of organizations and agencies working in defined geographic locations. These partnerships focused on areas of countryside which did not fit within the existing national framework of designated sites such as the National Parks or the more common Areas of Outstanding Natural Beauty (AONBs). All locations were distinct and had special landscape characteristics. Within such areas there existed a clear need to raise the bar on conservation and protection to complement the already recognized heritage value. Additionally, in awarding partnership funding, the criteria also included the presence of an existing range of active voluntary organizations engaged in countryside management, education and engagement. In Bedfordshire the Greensand County Landscape Partnership, (GCLP), which included Ampthill Great Park, was awarded grant-funding by HLF to work across a swathe of distinctive countryside dominated by the geological feature of the Greensand Ridge.

The key approach of these new bodies was to promote 'partnerships', which required the engagement of landowners, business enterprises, the established conservation agencies and the general public. Awards were made on the basis of submissions that demonstrated the distinctive landscape characteristics, but equally important, the presence of an existing array of local-interest groups which could be forged into a working partnership. The argument was that the best way to achieve a sustainable future was to deepen the historic and cultural links of people with their local landscape. The working assumption was that the public would be more interested and ready to identify with a known historical figure or national event. In Ampthill Park a historical event, such as the detention of Catherine of Aragon or the landscape gardening of Capability Brown, resonates with the public and is therefore more useful in promoting conservation than trying to conserve a rare insect or plant species.

The cultural connections then became a gateway to achieving other goals, including the restoration of threatened habitats such as lowland heath, ancient woodlands or parklands. These Partnerships have been successful nationally in mobilizing local interest and strengthening voluntary organizations in the expectation that essentially local efforts would outlive the Partnership funding from a finite lottery grant. This offered a degree of sustainability to both habitats and rural communities. Therefore, from the outset, all the Landscape Partnerships worked to identify heritage values which would be recognized by local people, and to use these as a bridge to achieving greater public engagement. A guiding principle was to enhance public interest in the countryside generally, and then move this interest to a more active phase of volunteering, training and the empowering of conservation interest groups, all of which would underwrite a sustainable future for an area of habitat value.

However, a recent change in emphasis has moved the focus from the heritage value of an entire landscape to that of a specific individual site. The visitor numbers attracted by the medieval castle win out over the cultural assemblage within a wider landscape. The concept of a Landscape Partnership initiative may have been something of a high-water mark in this wider approach to conservation thinking at landscape scale. This more recent tendency to move 'heritage' into a separate category misses the counterargument that the heritage industry needs to be rooted within landscape; that is, 'heritage getting its hands dirty'. The medieval castle was likely built of local stone and the quarries may still be visible; the building utilized timber from nearby ancient woodlands, which may still be intact; food was supplied from open fields ploughed in strips, which are apparent in the local pastures; and the fish ponds that supplied an important part of the diet can often still be found with some careful topographic research. In the same way, conservation sites such as ancient woodland are best understood within a landscape. Present-day nature reserves may have resulted from former extraction-industry activity such as peat-digging or chalk-quarrying. The Landscape Partnerships made these connections, linking conservation with the historical narrative.

The Kingdom of Mourne: a cultural landscape

The special character of this compact area of northeast Ireland is derived from the granite geology, leading to a rugged landscape. The topography has led to an area of small family owned farms. Previously isolated the Mournes are rich in folk lore and have a long cultural tradition. (Photography by Aileen Irvine}.

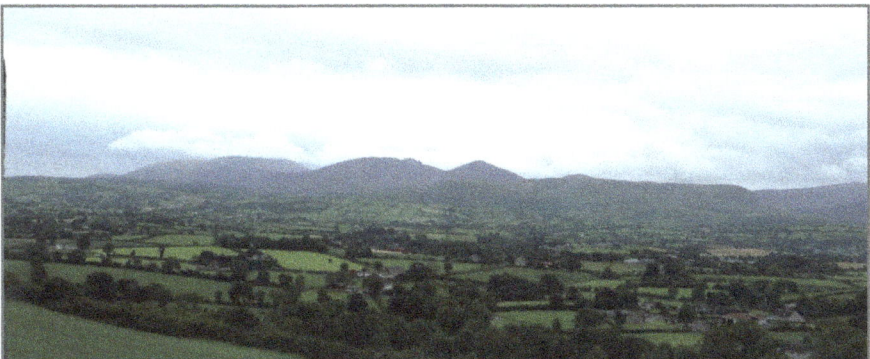

One example are the Mourne Mountains in Northern Ireland now also part of a Landscape Partnership. Within this discrete area, defined by its geology, the human history of the area is rooted in the granite rocks and the quarrying industry. Why was this rock so important as a building stone? What does this geology teach us about the vegetation? How does it differ from the surrounding rocks and how did its impact on land use, agriculture and settlement? These questions view heritage as bedding into the landscape, not floating above it.

National Parks and other public bodies that depend on the footfall of visitor numbers to support conservation have recognized that public engagement is heightened if the landscape can be explained and linked to a historical narrative. Engagement through 'storytelling' has become a part of the heritage business and has captured public imagination. The route into such a narrative is often straightforward and woven into the landscape thanks to an existing strong sense of local history. The tin-mining industry of Cornwall and the Roman occupation of Hadrian's Wall have left a very clear stamp on the land and both have a distinctive historical narrative. Other landscapes require more effort to tease out the stories. Local people will always be interested in a narrative which connects them to the area in which they live, and this can be expanded into the recording of local history in the same way that detailed wildlife-recording and archiving bring an area to life. Additionally, heritage links are now regarded as the touchstone in marketing and development a brand that will attract visitors. Where would Nottingham be without Robin Hood?

Secrets of the High Woods

In Sussex, the South Downs National Park launched such a project based on the less well-known forested areas of the park. Beneath the ancient woodlands of West Sussex is a historic landscape scattered with traces of the generations who have worked and lived there. As the National Park website reports, the task was to recover a lost landscape now hidden by the trees.[2]

The key to unlocking these hidden histories was an airborne survey using a remote sensing device known as LiDAR, (Light Detection and Ranging), which uses light beams and has the potential to penetrate gaps in the woodland canopy and so record the ground surface under the trees. This can reveal features that would not otherwise be seen. Combined with diligent map and archive research, many hours of fieldwork in the area and the collection of taped oral-history accounts, the project has collected large amounts of information and collated these into an absorbing account of woodland history. The method followed was, initially, a close examination of the radar imagery, which revealed many features previously unrecorded on the published maps. These clues were followed up by field exploration and archive research of old documents and maps. Finally, for more recent history, local people with a long-term connection to the woodland were interviewed by specially trained volunteers. The outcome is an extraordinary collection of archaeological and historical discoveries which enhances the understanding of the area and explains the landscape history. Published in a book entitled *Secrets of the High*

Woods, this project brought to light ancient field patterns, lost Roman roads, and more recently, an unexploded Second-World-War bomb.[3]

In June 2020, archaeologists reported another major discovery close to Stonehenge in Wiltshire. Excavations revealed very large pits, 10 metres in diameter and around 5 metres deep, spaced at regular intervals and in a circle. This landscape has long been protected and the Stonehenge and Avebury Megalithic Cultural Landscape is designated as one of international importance. The archaeological monuments are set in a distinctive rolling chalk landscape, which continues to reveal surprising discoveries. The recent revelations add another layer to this sacred landscape and explain the urgency of protection to facilitate future exploration.[4]

There is space for a contrary view, such as that of Robert Hewison, who published a book in 1987, which was very critical of the emerging preoccupation with heritage. This, he argued, was becoming a national obsession with the past. His title makes the point directly. *The Heritage Industry: Britain in a Climate of Decline* is a plea to protect the present and the future from, 'a creeping takeover by the past'.[5] In the thirty years since publication the emphasis on historical sites has continued to grow. The EU-funded agricultural subsidy schemes, both at basic and higher levels, encouraged the conservation of features such as medieval ridge-and-furrow plough marks and archaeological monuments. Features already designated as Scheduled Ancient Monuments which are considered to have national importance are protected by law.

Many such features are also protected by designations such as being within a National Park, where stricter planning guidelines apply. The difficulty comes when changes are considered necessary by farmers and land managers, in order to remain economically competitive. Although it may be possible to protect an area of cultural heritage, the price can be farm businesses changing radically or leaving farming entirely. This then pushes the present rural economy into a holding role as a steward of the past. The dilemma is very real where profits are marginal, the climate and topography are unfavourable and the farming population is ageing. Are we willing, or is it healthy, to simply pay people to be stewards of a past environment?

The National Trust is actively seeking to find such a balance and acknowledges that ordinary details of the landscape such as stone walls are often taken for granted until they need repair, and such everyday features such as hedges make for local distinctiveness. Although the Trust is keen to ensure the economic viability of the land, this is only possible with carefully designed national subsidies which can provide a basic income: these then give the margin required for additional conservation measures. The late cutting of hay to allow birds to nest can be encouraged, but only if there is a favourable subsidy regime to make a decent livelihood in the first place.

A changing landscape

A gas-powered power station under construction, in the flat landscape of the Marston Vale, Bedfordshire. This image illustrates the dynamic nature of land. (photograph by Vaughan Dean)

The argument then comes full circle. Public funds paid to achieve public goods are to be applauded, but there will be some losers along the path to a different countryside. Any future swing towards a farming regime that encourages wildlife, or enhances the appearance of the uplands at the expense of fewer grazing animals and therefore less profit, will need to be financially underwritten and supported as a 'public good'. In Chapter 1 we saw that the forthcoming Environment Land Management (ELMS) framework promised by the Government proposed just such a trade-off. The challenge is how to work out the details of what can be achieved at the farm level, and therefore funded by tax and, at the same time, still enable the farmer or landowner to make a decent livelihood. The other side of the trade-off also will require intensive farming to be even more commercial and perhaps less 'nature-friendly'. The pushback against this should not be underestimated. Often it surfaces in the local and regional farming press, with headlines like 'Giving up land is sacrilege', and quotes such as, 'Northumberland is a heartland for livestock farming and it has a future - otherwise food will run out', common in the letters and comment pages.[6]

* * *

At the heart of this balancing act is our relationship with the land. Are we sufficiently interested and willing to pay for the upkeep of these cultural places with a rich history? If these places and landscapes are bound to our cultural identity then how can this be recognized without restricting the livelihoods of the people who live and work there? In addition to the understanding that cultural landscapes have a place nationally and are important elements of identity and history, is there space for these areas to continue to offer opportunity and employment? This means allowing forms of land use and agriculture that are not disruptive and intrusive: planting the Stonehenge countryside with new woodlands, on the basis that they would have a beneficial impact on carbon storage, is as problematic as erecting a theme park in the shadow of the stones.

The above are both national and personal questions. Although the idea of heritage and cultural landscapes is now firmly enshrined in policy, these places are also personal to a great extent. Every place contains an accumulated store of past experiences: some are national events; other very personal. But what makes a place special? Is it possible to distil the 'spirit of a place', and can this be more than a branding and marketing idea aimed at visitors?

Meanwhile a question which has been avoided since the Domesday Book revolves around who owns this land and whether the conservation of cultural or distinctive landscapes can be achieved with land prices at such high levels. Since the rising price of land is driven by investment interests rather than farming, how can conservation, public access and the preservation of any cultural landscapes be protected or, better still, enhanced?

CHAPTER SEVEN

The Oldest, Darkest, Best-Kept Secret

During Christmas 1085, William the Conqueror held council with his court at Gloucester. The decision was made that the king needed to know more about the land of England: who owned what and where; how much was the land worth; and what was it was used for. The motive was clear: the king needed to increase his tax revenue and understand more about his barons. He was anxious to know the value of their estates and the character of land in England. Understand your enemy or potential enemy. The court recorded that:

> *After this the King held a large meeting, and very deep consultation with his council, about this land; how it was occupied, and by what sort of men. Then sent he his men over all England into each shire; commissioning them to find out, how may hundreds of hides were in the shire, what land the King himself had and what stock upon the land; or what dues he ought to have by the year from the shire.* [2]

The findings were brought together into what we now know as the Domesday Book, and this record provides a unique insight into the thirty-one counties of England between the Channel and the River Tees. Completed at an astonishing pace during 1086, the Domesday Book is the first public record of land, providing the new Norman bureaucracy with essential tax information on Saxon England. Although the main purpose of the Domesday survey was to report on ownership and land values, an interesting element for the modern reader is the detail this survey provides into late eleventh-century use of land across most of England. So, we learn not only the area of land used for arable cultivation, but can see that an assessment was also made of the potential capability for more land to be ploughed; the extent of meadow land used for grazing; and a measure of woodland, calculating how many pigs this could support. This audit of England provides a unique insight into medieval ownership and land use.

The spur for this gigantic effort was the power of information: a database which allowed the gathering of taxes. Not until concerns over food security in the early and mid-twentieth century was there another systematic and comprehensive effort mobilized to understand the character and potential of land. In the 1930s a massive land-use survey across all of Britain – largely undertaken by school pupils – was done under the direction of Professor of Geography, Dudley Stamp.[3] This was later augmented by a wartime National Farm Survey to assess the supply of vital food during the period of rationing and threat of invasion. The latter survey reported on all farms over 5 acres and covered 99 per cent of all the agricultural land in both England and Scotland. Both of these twenty-century audits provide rare insights into the land and how it was being used at a time of heightened food-security concerns.

Since these wartime efforts, any interest in land use has been very much left to the planners. Public interest has been relegated at a local level to occasional flurries of concern over a road alignment or the removal of a few trees. At the national level, the National Infrastructure Commission deals with large planning issues, such as HS2 and future airport expansion. Public consultations have been mounted prior to both local and national developments, but the power to really shift the agenda has proved to be limited. However, the looming climatic emergency, coupled with concern over the dependence on imported food – especially regarding food supply in the aftermath of Brexit and the Covid-19 pandemic – may just reignite interest. In the early months of 2020, the term 'land use', appeared to be making a comeback in the media. There are earnest discussions in relation to tree-planting, the storing of carbon, reductions in flooding and the new concept of 'ecological services' provided by the countryside. The routing of the HS2 line has become as important as the economic case for construction. A press release by the Woodland Trust in early 2020, was unambiguous and brought the issue of land back to the centre of debate:

> *Right now, the biggest single threat from development to ancient woodland is the HS2 rail project. Up and down the country, ancient woods and trees face the axe to make way for the high-speed train line. Despite a lengthy review process, Government announced on 11 February 2020 that the project will still go ahead.*[4]

The relevance of this debate over land will only intensify as decisions are required on public spending around farm-subsidy priorities, the part played by land in carbon storage, the conservation of wildlife and increases in biodiversity, and the planting of new woodland.

During both the medieval period and also in the mid-1900s, especially in time of war, land-based surveys went beyond the simple question of what the land was being used for and asked the big questions: Who owns this land? And who manages this patch of England? Therefore, the medieval Domesday Book for the Bedfordshire estates records that the largest owner was the king, followed by two Norman bishops and then a Nigel d'Aubigny, from the Bayeux area of France. Landholdings were then granted to followers including, at the village of Silsoe, the mistress of D'Aubigny, noted in the Domesday Book as 'in Silsoe a certain concubine of Nigel holds two hides'.[5]

The title of this chapter is taken from a book by Guy Shrubsole, who explains in some detail how land ownership became such a secretive issue. One interesting attempt to shine a light on the ownership was made in Victorian times and the outcome of this survey, *The Return of Owners of Land* (1873–75), was compiled by checking statistics already available. After a delay the results became, for a time, a political issue which was rapidly snuffed out when the answers were considered unpalatable.[1]

A property-owning democracy: lessons from history

There are a number of reasons why historical insight provides pointers to the use of land across modern Britain. The Domesday Book survey of the counties of England, sketched briefly at the beginning of this chapter, provided William the Conqueror with a strategic view of his kingdom. This was then a powerful tool to be used to extract taxes and keep a grip on power. There was no further serious questioning of the overall distribution of land parcelled out following the Norman Conquest, until a groundswell of disquiet surfaced 800 years later during the Victorian Era. The problem was crystallized clearly in a parliamentary speech by a major landowner who asked the Government in February 1872:

> Whether it is the intention of this government to take steps for ascertaining accurately the number of Proprietors of Land or Houses in the United Kingdom, with the quantity of land owned by each?

Lord Derby went on to state this would be a public service for, 'currently there was a great outcry about what was called the monopoly of land.[6] Remarkably, the Government of the day quickly instituted a review entitled, *Return of Owners of Land.* This became a vast bureaucratic exercise to collate thousands of existing records. John Bateman, a country squire, collated these for owners of over 3,000 acres, in a book called *The Acre-Ocracy of England.*[7] The outcome was explosive, adding fuel to the pressure for radical land reform.

The headline from this survey was that just over 4,000 families owned just over 50 per cent of the country and 95 per cent of the population owned no land at all. Bateman's work became a bestseller running to four editions and several updates between 1876 and 1883. In the election which followed in 1885, the slogan was *'Three acres and a cow'* – a popular rallying call from campaigners seeking land reform.

However, the outcome was an anticlimax with the only significant change being the Allotment Act of 1887. Politics moved on and the moment was lost.

In 1909, Winston Churchill raised the issue once again and remarkably advocated a land tax of 20 per cent on the unearned increase in land values, but this floundered once more on the need for a registry of all landholdings. All the good intentions were then quickly swallowed up by the First World War. Proposed changes in the planning system brought forward in mid-2020 have again raised these questions. An economist would describe this as the challenge of a 'long-term land-value capture policy', which is complicated terminology for a tax on land profits. The controversial nature of this should never be underestimated.

These historical failures and others serve to underline several serious points. Firstly, a pattern of ancient land ownership has survived almost intact, with land as an asset owned by a remarkably small number of families – a stubborn riposte to the idea of a 'property-owning democracy'. Secondly, the land issue is divisive politically and any government faces the question with trepidation. A crusading politician kicks over the anthill of land ownership at their peril. It has yet to be proven that there are votes in land reform.

Just as the ownership of his kingdom was important to William in 1086, this debate on ownership has again surfaced recently, as the question of land managed in the public interest has gained momentum. Guy Shrubsole asks this question in *Who owns England?* – his book of the same title.[1] Bringing together an array of statistical sources, he attempts to tease out some answers and shine light on the present ownership pattern in England. The headline result, which demonstrates that only 25,000 individuals or companies own over half of England, is an echo of the Victorian survey on ownership, with half the land concentrated in a few families or companies. The Country Land and Business Association also reflects this skewed pattern, with around 50 per cent of all land in England and Wales owned by its 35,000 members.[10] For many centuries there has been a stubborn pattern of resisting change.

Keep out: trespassers will be prosecuted … but not often

From the strange unbalanced picture of land ownership in England it is only a quick hop across a wall, ignoring the 'Private Land' notices, to tackling the issue of trespass on land and breaking the law as it stands. In a powerful new book, Nick Hayes turns a spotlight on this fraught topic, and *The Book of Trespass* begins with the startling fact that at present 92 per cent of all land in England is inaccessible to the public, with an equally high proportion of waterways also barred from public access.[8]

The author makes the point that the law, as framed in the Countryside and Rights of Way legislation of 2000, is designed to allow a landowner redress if there is damage to land or property. Trespass cases are rare in courts and are usually to settle boundary disputes. However, this will change if Government decides to toughen the law and elevate trespass to a criminal offence.

The book is an opening salvo in a campaign to 'lift the spell' of private ownership, which rules out vast tracts of land which are closed to the public. This is not only in individual private hands, but also owned and managed by the National Trust, the water companies and other public bodies.[9]

The author references the historic trespass campaign in the 1930s, which led to the mass trespass on Kinder Scout in 1933. This act of mass civil disobedience did lead to more access and ultimately resulted in the formation of the National Parks.

Earlier chapters stressed the point that the issues of climate change, wildlife protection, food supply and flood prevention will all have a direct and immediate impact on future generations in the UK. A more innovative approach to how we manage the countryside and landscape is central to any coping strategy. The continuation of 'business as usual' cannot be considered a satisfactory approach. All the signals are that public concern is leading Government towards some truly innovative thinking, which has been massively underscored by the recovery plans and ideas being suggested to lead the UK into a post-pandemic world. Many such plans have advocated a green revolution or a green-led recovery, with greater engagement with healthy food, food security and the availability of food for all. It is remarkable that the issue of land and how it can be used to fulfil these intentions has not entered the debate at this time of change.

It is clear that the question of how to influence the future use of land will inevitably come back to disputes over ownership. Throughout Britain any proposed changes will eventually bump up against this issue. Ambitious and widely supported efforts which aim to tackle carbon storage by increased tree-planting, the encouragement of wildlife or improved public access all hinge on agreements with land owners.

Direct Government leverage on the use of land has steadily declined as the trend over several decades has been for land to move out of public ownership and into private hands. Despite conservation charities such as the National Trust purchasing strategic sites with specific habitats or special landscape value, the balance has shifted. Public land –council farms, school sports fields, Ministry of Defence sites and sites previously occupied by State industries – have all been sold out of public ownership. This must reduce any immediate influence over the way in which this land is used in the public interest. An interesting pushback against this tide to convert public land to private was an attempt to sell off the Forestry Commission estate in England, which was defeated by public opposition in 2013. The Government, responding to a report, reversed the intention to sell and described the forests in England as 'a public asset.'[11]

From a financial perspective, the logic behind the sale of public land is beyond question. Since 1995, the total value of UK land has increased fivefold: the investment value of land far outperforms all other sectors. The housing market fuels this dramatically, with average agricultural land prices in early 2019 rocketing from £20,000 per hectare to an eye- watering £6 million for land with the right to build.[12]

More recently, in the early months of 2020, the following advertisement ran in regional newspapers in the east of England: 'A superb commercial arable farm in Bedfordshire: asking price £8,950,000'. The key word here is 'commercial'. This is top-class land with a history of wheat production since Roman times and capable of growing a wide range of arable crops. Reflecting on the agricultural choices facing the Government, this land, and most of arable southern and eastern England, represents the heartland of grain production.

Any considerations of alternative use will be trumped by food-security concerns.[13]

Largest Lowland Farms on the Market 2017 & 2018

	County Size (in acres)	Guide price (£ million)	Price/acre
Lincolnshire	3,204	25,000,000	7,803
Suffolk	2,177	31,500,000	14,469
Leicestershire	1,737	13,500,000	7,772
North Yorkshire	1,665	16,500,000	9,910
Hampshire	1,523	22,250,000	14,609
West Yorkshire	1,363	15,000,000	11,005
Hertfordshire	1,349	19,000,000	14,085
Northumberland	1,232	4,500,000	3,653
Norfolk	1,200	11,000,000	9,167

In 2018, *Farmers Weekly* published the table above showing average asking prices for commercial land in lowland.[14] This illustrates the value of these large arable estates. Taking the cost and extent (903 acres), the price tag is broadly in line with the Farmland Index, at close to £10,000 per acre (i.e. £24,500 per hectare).

The prosperous south-east of England is always a target for potential housing development. One possible outcome of the pandemic is an emerging trend for working from home rather than the conventional office, together with a drift away from London. Developers are banking on people investing in more space, both within the home and in the countryside which is accessible to green space. This makes the proposed Oxford-to-Cambridge Arc a critical corridor across the centre of England. A million new homes together with the supporting infrastructure will be required. The scale of this new development makes the investment of millions of pounds in land a low risk. The historic steady rise in agricultural prices year on year is likely to continue, alongside the potential windfall of some land, perhaps on the agricultural margins, sold for housing.

There are many discussion points for politicians to ponder in relation to the demand for housing and land, and the historical context is relevant here. The radical 1947 Town and Country Planning Act, enacted under the Attlee Government, allowed local authorities to acquire land for development at 'existing use values', but there was no premium if it was earmarked for development. The expanding city of Milton Keynes illustrates this well. The unserviced land cost was around 1 per cent of the finished house. Today the cost of land with permission to build is approaching 50 per cent. This is an issue which has been with us for some time. In 1909, in a 'people's budget', Churchill promoted a 'land tax' and his language was blunt: 'The landowner sits and does nothing', while his investment increases.15

Something has gone wrong with the land market which is often described as *dysfunctional*. If other goals for the countryside, especially in relation to the aspirations for an outcome which could be called a 'public good', are to be realized, then bold and potentially disruptive actions are required. As mentioned, this is politically contested terrain as highlighted in the title for this chapter. Any land reform is guaranteed to raise the political temperature and is beyond the scope of this book.

The implication however is clear: the scope for major changes in how the land is used is presently constrained. If there is a determination to alter the mix of land use in a highly populated country, then there are fundamental changes required, which challenge our values in relation to the land, landscapes and nature. 'A superb commercial arable farm', as described by the vendors for the Bedfordshire farm, is an investment and any interventions will be viewed in the light of returns on the capital expended. This is land for production. These arable farms are often portrayed as *essential* for the nation's food security, which returns the debate to the balance of production versus conservation and biodiversity versus yield. The optimum size for such farms that require substantial investment in machinery and the technology to guarantee high yields, has been increasing steadily. The era of megafarms more often associated with the USA is imminent in the UK.

Invest and buy land: the rise of the megafarm

The idea of the megafarm does not sit easily with public perception of the British countryside; it is more Kansas than Kent, and not the stuff of *Countryfile's* Sunday evening viewing. However, the trend towards larger farms has been creeping steadily upwards for some time and fifteen years ago there were nine times as many small farms as today, and greater variety in the types of farms. The proposed changes in the delivery of farm subsidies will fund the landowner's improvements to the environment and also encourage increased yields and productivity, needed to maintain food security. But will both of these strands be paid for, and how will any environmental improvements be measured?

If you google 'Which is the biggest farm in England?' the answer is given as the Elveden Estate in Norfolk at 22,500 acres, of which 10,000 ha is owned by the Guinness family. The average farm size in Kansas is close to 800 acres. Field sizes at Elveden are in the range of 100 acres each, well suited to modern, powerful farm equipment. The farm on the sandy soils of the Norfolk Breckland specializes in potatoes, onions, carrots and parsnips, all crops which are often irrigated. The estate website carries separate pages on the ongoing investment made in maintaining biodiversity and farm operations in an environmentally friendly way.[16] The estate employs a full-time conservation officer and is an example of a commercial arable farm at the heart of efforts to secure UK food security, at pains to move to nature-friendly farming.

The uptake of land by companies, both UK- and overseas-registered, can now be documented and amounts to about 18 per cent of land in England and Wales. Large commercial arable farms coming on to the market are advertised as multifaceted investment opportunities. Commercial production requires efficient operations, including the precision application of fertilizer, tight labour costings, large fields and bigger machinery. Can this be married to environment-friendly farming? Will the new payments system ensure that wildlife is considered at the expense of yields? Is it possible to design a payment system to protect nature and make also make a profit? [17]

In the livestock sector, as is often the case, *The Archers* BBC Radio programme spotted this trend of investing in single-enterprise megafarms some time ago. Borchester Land set out to create a 'mega-dairy', with 1,500 cattle all housed indoors in special sheds. This was to become the profit centre for the 1,000-acre estate, which also had a lowland pheasant shoot. Not surprisingly, this met substantial local opposition in Ambridge.

Elsewhere, the largest growth has been in the poultry sector with close to 1,500 permits granted for these large single-enterprise operations. At the top end there is potential for processing one million chickens each week. Concerns here are over waste disposal, and the cost of importation of imported grain and soya as feedstock. Paradoxically, the consumer demand for free-range eggs and chicken raised outdoors has added to pollution problems. Large flocks produce waste on the land, which then washes off into waterways following heavy rain. Again, the balance of the environment and cheap food may come into conflict. Expect a few feathers to fly.

An agribusiness landscape

The large field farming landscapes of the south and east of England are at the centre of any debate on food security. Any changes to the payment of farm support, and moves towards nature-friendly farming will need to take account of the harvest from these fields. The uncertain spring and hot summer of 2020 saw yields fall and the year on year increase in productivity can no longer be guaranteed.

Scientists, policymakers and agriculturalists have been thinking through how to achieve a possible balance between the commercial farm sector and wildlife for some time. One of the forward thinkers is Fred Pearce, a science writer who described the options as either 'land sharing' or 'land sparing'. He puts the argument as follows:

Should we be sharing our landscapes with nature by reviving small woodlands and adopting small-scale eco-friendly farming? Or should we instead be sparing large tracts of land for nature's exclusive use – by creating more national parks and industrializing agriculture on existing farmland.[18]

The subsidy frameworks were already easing farmers and landowners towards the ideas of sharing land with nature in a variety of ways. The existing Higher-Level Stewardship Scheme rewarded conservation gains, providing support for wider field headlands, planting trees in field corners, delays in hedge-cutting to encourage nesting birds and changes in the drainage of uplands to restore wetlands. This was not quite business as usual, but a managed transition which increased the foothold of biodiversity and conservation within a farming landscape. These agreements were for a defined period and not all were renewed. There was a risk that a farm manager could decide enough was enough and drop out so any benefits would be lost. Within the new radical proposed ELMS framework for farm support, both large-scale commercial, intensive farms and more traditional farm businesses will be encouraged and rewarded to make available space for nature to recover over longer time periods. Will this be adequate?

The small-scale interventions which have already been implemented have had a limited effect, but the lobby for the bolder ideas of 'land sparing' are more strident. This is a radical approach requiring a complete move away from commercial farming in limited areas, with well-defined nature or wildness reserves that would provide the necessary habitat for the recovery of biodiversity. The message from the 'wilding' advocates is that anything else is just *tinkering at the edges*. The *WildEast* experiment in eastern England and the Knapp Estate wilding initiatives are indications that these ideas are taking root. In her book, Isabella Tree described how a previously arable farm struggling with difficult clay soils was gradually allowed to revert and the difficulties this raised with conventional thinking of what was expected from a farm.[19] The abandonment of traditional arable cultivation with tidy fields offended many neighbouring farmers, who were deeply committed to stewardship of the land, and for whom watching fields overrun with ragwort then scrub was difficult. Part of the new business model for the estate includes attracting people interested in wildlife as a form of 'nature tourism'.

During the first half of 2020 visits to the countryside multiplied, with many people discovering or rediscovering the pleasure of watching the spring unfold and move into summer. Bicycle sales soared and families explored local areas both on- and off-road, and the public footpath network was well used. However, not all farmers and land owners were delighted with this surge in interest. The idea of adding people to the mix of intensive farming is not always welcome. Nevertheless, there is a growing appetite for the outdoors and this will have an inevitable impact on how the countryside is managed. Can a balance be achieved in an investment climate where land is very much seen as a private or commercial asset demanding a return?

Renewable energy – a new use for land

Power generated from wind and solar sources overtook the use of electricity from fossil fuels for a short period in early 2019 and by the second half of 2020 renewables were contributing just short of 50 per cent of power generation, with coal powered stations less than one per cent of the UK energy mix. Solar arrays and on-shore wind farms together all require access to land, which can in many cases remain in grazing use. (Photograph by Richard Revels)

CHAPTER EIGHT

Breathing Spaces

The supermarket noticeboard advertised both weekly 'Well-being Walks' over a five-week period, next to 'Well-being Runs' over the same duration. The need to diversify has led farmers to arrange farm runs at the weekend around the edge of muddy fields, and the spiritual dimension is not neglected, with active 'faith walks' arranged by religious groups. The 'Park Run' movement has taken off in Britain with thousands joining regular runs against the clock in an effort to exceed a 'personal best'. Doctors are encouraging patients to garden and walk, and concerns around mental-health issues have led to the recognition of the outdoors as an important health benefit. The UK Government has made this a centrepiece of the 25-year Environment Bill, as set out in the most recent progress report of May 2019.

> *Our 25-Year Environment Plan was drawn up in recognition of this moral, ethical and also economic imperative: in a healthy environment, we too are healthier, and also happier and more productive* [1]

Suddenly, the connection of health, well-being and the environment has returned with a sharper focus than ever before. Lifestyle and health messages have moved beyond the weekly yoga class and 'you are what you eat' slogans to embrace the benefits of the outdoors. To achieve this there is an obvious requirement for a welcoming countryside which is accessible, close by and free or at minimal cost. Other challenges include broadening the range of people who are interested and willing to visit rural locations. Conservation organizations worry that they have a membership and audience which is middle-class, white, lacks diversity and presently feels comfortable in the countryside. The challenge is to move beyond this core to attract a new more diverse audience.

The increasing body of knowledge backed by solid research findings – that the availability of green spaces does improve health outcomes – makes the task of attracting people to the outdoors more urgent. The difficulty comes in attempting to work out benefits which can be utilized to attach a value to outdoor spaces in general and, specifically, to the countryside. Economists have been wrestling with these numbers and a charity, Fields in Trust, has bravely suggested a saving to the NHS of £111 million a year.[2] The ambitious aim of this charity is to ensure that 75 per cent of the UK population is within a 10-minute walk of a protected park by 2022.

Placing an economic value on green space is difficult with regard to direct health benefits and becomes even more complicated when there is an attempt to quantify 'well-being'. Undeterred, Fields in Trust conclude that an economic value can be based on both physical and mental health and this can be related to periods spent outdoors. Using a UK representative sample, they estimated that both well-being and self-reported general health are significantly higher for frequent park and green space users compared to non-users, and this was then given a value at around £30 per year for each individual. This is an important guide when combined with other information and can be used when targeting investment, especially in urban areas.

The understanding that contact with nature has a positive effect on health and well-being is not new. The Victorian ideal of fresh air and exercise as a 'cure-all' still lingers: Florence Nightingale remarked that patients who did not have any natural light, 'endured the most acute suffering'. The benefits of contact with the outdoors, especially on mental health, have inspired a recent flood of books which tackle this topic in a helpful way. Two examples with apt titles illustrate this publishing trend: Isabel Hardman's *The Natural Health Service: What the Great Outdoors can do for your Mind*, and Emma Mitchell's *The Wild Remedy: How Nature Mends Us – A Diary,* both describe how the authors, struggling with physical and mental-health problems, were restored by regular exposure to and learning about the natural world.[3] These writers and many more went well beyond a casual walk in the park. The road to recovery included systematic observations and an active effort to understand the process of recovery. The mental-health charity Mind describes this as 'making efforts to connect, to take notice, to give, to keep learning, and to be active'.

However, there are limits to what has been described as 'Green Prozac' and no shortage of scepticism and debunking. The journalist Patrick Barkham attempts to provide a balance, pointing out that the people who earn a livelihood working with nature and being outdoors as a living are not immune from depression.[4] Indeed, farmers as a group are prone to mental illness, with a suicide rate recorded as one death every week in the industry.[5]

The title of this book – *How to Value a Skylark* –reflects these uncertainties. Placing an economic value on the natural world, represented in the title by the skylark, and the individual's enjoyment of the environment is a hazardous task. How much would you pay for access to your local park? Can we really measure the effect of an ancient wood on well-being? And how does this rank in value with the impact that the woodland may have on the occurrence of downstream floods? This is a long way from a simple calculation to find the market value of the standing timber.

Inherent in these assessments is both the practical difficulty of agreeing a price and, more broadly, an ethical debate on market economics being applied to nature and then given a monetary value. This is not only an economic argument, but cuts to the centre of how we feel about placing nature in the marketplace. George Monbiot has made the point that the calculation of a price implies the possibility of lining something up for sale, in which case the exercise is sinister, or it is not for sale, in which case it is meaningless. The cost is only sensible if the item is for sale. Underlying this argument is that the public is more open to emotional and ethical arguments than to pure economic costs and benefits.[6] Many conservation organizations and economists working to reach assessments of value recognize that placing a value on the natural world is an imperfect tool, but they have to start somewhere. They argue that 'gaps' in valuation will reduce over time and that they are moving in the right direction.

***

In Bedfordshire, these valuation techniques have been applied in order to assess the 'stock of natural capital' within one county. The Bedfordshire Local Nature Partnership has been gathering data to implement an audit of the stock of environmental assets. Significantly, this assessment will include a calculation of both recreational and welfare services, plus the gains to physical health provided by access to the countryside. The information will be used in planning developments associated with the Oxford-to-Cambridge Arc of new infrastructure. It is estimated that treating mental ill-health costs an estimated £690 million in lost productivity annually, so finding a way to take account of well-being and mental health in any economic valuation is important.[7] The stark figure often quoted is that one person in four will suffer some form of mental-health issue during their lifetime. The part played by access to green space, nature and the countryside in preventing and treating these problems has now become a respected academic topic.[8] Although medical researchers explore the links between the environment and health, economists struggle with the concept of price and value attached to habitats.

Footpaths and bridle ways-the escape route to the countryside

During the period of lockdown in early 2020 there was marked increase in the use of public access paths with a substantial increase in off road cycling. The maintenance of these paths falls to local government which often struggles with the resources required to look after a large path network in England and Wales. Rambler groups are an important force in helping to keep these vital leisure paths open and well maintained.

Well-being enters the mainstream

During the Covid-19 pandemic the mental-health benefits of spending time in green space in the outdoors was brought sharply into focus. Nature offered a much-needed escape from lockdown and the well-being of children became a particular concern. Many children who have access to gardens and green space have benefited from an outdoor learning experience and there was an expectation that when a new school term was launched the outdoor learning experience would become fully integrated into school timetables. A *Wild for Life,* movement offered web-based schooling experiences to complement the formal school curriculum and was aimed especially at children aged 4 to 11 years. The popularity of 'Forest Schools' continues to grow, offering children freedom and opportunities for creative play in woodland.

Aware of this rising interest in access to countryside and urban green space, the Heritage Community Fund commissioned a report on how to maximize the benefits of being outside and in touch with nature.

The Space to Thrive report published in 2020 reinforced the physical, mental-health and well-being outcomes, and helped to crystallize thinking on how best to meet demand and what people most value.

The results highlight some interesting surprises. The condition of parks and any green space is important; surprisingly, more so than the actual number. The importance of activating local involvement in any design, to foster a sense of ownership, was stressed: the best results were always when a community was encouraged to be actively engaged and learn from nature. Parks therefore have become a social asset and require investment in community involvement, as well as the usual physical maintenance. Numerous 'Friends of the Park' type schemes bring together volunteers, schools and community groups to ensure parks are well used and also kept in good condition.[9]

From well-being and mental health, it is a short step to the spiritual refreshment offered by nature and the countryside. The popular BBC Radio programme *Ramblings* recognized this in 2013, with a whole series entitled *Walking for Spiritual Renewal*, which explored how different faith groups approached nature by being outside and walking in a group. One programme on offer included a lesson 'on the art of walking silently', which may be a challenge for a radio programme! Local faith walks and more ambitious long-distance pilgrimages are now popular, often reaching audiences which are difficult to connect with. The British Pilgrimage Trust offers a menu of pilgrim routes usually dedicated to local saints.

In Bedfordshire, the linking of interfaith gatherings and conservation groups has claimed to deliver a health dividend. The Luton Council of Faiths and the Forestry Commission came together to address both social exclusion and health issues. A forest ranger led walks in local woodland with both mixed- and single-faith groups involved. This has demonstrated that an understanding of the environment can be combined with enjoyment and that over time social inclusion can be improved. Physical and mental-health benefits are also real.

All of these activities, from the ancient routes of pilgrims to children messing about in the woods, depend on access. The pilgrim routes across England follow ancient pathways now designated as public footpaths, and kept open by the combined efforts of local authorities and voluntary work parties arranged by ramblers' clubs.

The opportunities for children to have an adventure in the woods depend on access to woodland owned and managed by a public agency in some form. In this way the countryside has become an essential part of health and education and needs to be valued. The exact techniques of attaching a value to specific habitats and adding up the services provided – carbon storage, flood prevention, air-quality improvement and now health and well-being – are problematic. Perhaps, as argued by George Monbiot, this is a fallacy at best and dangerous at worst.

One of the foremost and most prolific nature writers of recent years has been Richard Mabey. His book, *Nature Cure*, is credited with being the first of the now many publications that chart the regenerative impact of nature. Following a period of mental illness, he found time spent in the Chiltern Hills and Norfolk allowed him space and perspective to recover. In an earlier book, *Common Ground*, he described the place of nature as, 'to renew the living fabric of the land so that it replenishes the spirits of its inhabitants'. It is pertinent to note here that the full title of the 2005 book is *Common Ground: A Place for Nature in Britain's Future?* The presence of the question mark is significant![10]

In attempting to describe people's attachment to landscape and countryside, phrases such as 'a sense of place' or 'a spirit of place' are often used. There is little doubt that topography, climate and geology, combined with the landscape history of human activity, all contribute to make an area distinctive – even unique.

CHAPTER NINE

A Sense of Place

In 2019, I had the good fortune to rent a traditional Dutch house on the north-east corner of the city of Utrecht. Across the street was a waterway described by the locals as a '*sloot*'. A *sloot*, in the hierarchy of Dutch waterways, is much less important than a canal, and even lower than an urban '*gracht*', which is common in most Dutch towns and lends a picturesque addition to the townscapes of the Netherlands. This 15-metre-wide *sloot* was built as a defence line joining nineteenth-century fortifications to deter invaders, and marked the boundary of the old city from the polder beyond.

The polder is the most distinctive of Dutch landscapes and is imbedded in the identity and modern way of life of the nation. On the edge of densely crowded urban space, this is where people come to walk, jog, fish, ride horses, picnic, birdwatch, and teach children to cycle before they are trusted in the town. Polders are also, of course, a valued farming resource, which have contributed to the intensive and highly successful Dutch farming sector. These polders may be flat and at first hold little interest for the visitor from Britain. It takes some time to become accustomed to the wide skies which press down on the view. The backdrop of a windmill or a church spire in the distance is needed to add perspective to the tree-lined dykes and neat farms. To the Dutch, these polders are not only symbols of the struggle against flooding and invaders, but are now valued spaces to be celebrated. City people watch eagerly for the arrival of the storks in the spring, and wildfowl in the winter. This is a landscape not just familiar but carries with it a unique 'sense of place', which is celebrated in the Dutch school of landscape painting and is rooted in Dutch identity.

Throughout this book the emphasis has been on the practical and tangible aspects of the changes which are likely to impact the countryside in Britain. More trees, different crops, connected and better-managed nature reserves will all make a positive difference. However, it is also important to recognize the intangible feelings and atmosphere which make a place special and distinctive. Then it becomes possible to unravel why some landscapes are cherished and memorable. This is often described as the 'spirit of place;, or 'the soul of a place', and is made up of memories, stories, rituals, festivals and traditional knowledge. Writers and artists have grappled with these ideas and tried to capture the essence of a place by using words like 'ambience' or 'atmosphere', which complement the straightforward geography.

These are all elusive ideas and that slide into folklore and legend. Nevertheless, there is a core understanding that place is important to people, well beyond the bold descriptions of geology and landscape. The analogy is often made with the atmosphere in an older building, such as a place of worship, which embraces more than architecture or acoustics: the layers of history combine with the physical attributes to make for a sense of character which is distinctive or even unique.

This distinctiveness is recognized at differing scales, from regional landscapes to a well-loved wood or stretch of coastline. Modern marketing has latched on to this and the branding industry has sold places such as the 'Jurassic Coast' of Dorset. Although the key component here may be the limestone geology, the attraction now thrives on local history, dinosaurs and a special landscape. The importance of conveying something distinctive and regional has always been a useful marketing tool, from beer to cheese. The challenge is to use a place to encourage visitors to think of it as different and distinctive; a place they want to return to.

This effort to capture and distil the power of place is not new. Roly Smith, in his book *A Sense of Place*, traces this search for distinctiveness back to the Latin, *genius loci,* or 'spirit of place'. His book brings together a series of essays described as 'the best of outdoor writing on the British landscape'. Many locations celebrated by the book's contributors are well known, such as the Lake District, whereas others are more obscure, such as the Greensand Ridge of the Weald in Kent.[2] Often, remoteness adds to this mix of distinctiveness of place which is rich in local lore, with a feel of being different. One of the best examples of this are the granite hills in South Down in Northern Ireland. In a book which weaves together the geology, landscape, farming, quarrying, and a way of life, the author Estyn Evans paints a picture of how a relatively small area has, over millennia, become unique and special to many people throughout Ireland and beyond.[3] Folklore and legend – what the modern heritage industry would regard as valuable marketing material assets – are bound intimately into the image of uniqueness. However, this folk history is still alive and appreciated. A tale told by Evens in his book *Mourne Country* illustrates this legacy.

> *I recently asked a strong farmer in Mourne, why he troubled to plough round and did not remove a thorn tree on his land. He expressed scorn for all superstitions, but clearly was taking no risks, for as I was leaving, he called me back and offered £5 if I would get rid of the tree for him.*

These evocative descriptions of landscape and people rooted in a particular place have now become part of a growing body of literature which has managed to capture the distinctive character of a place. Writers with a talent for describing landscapes have been rediscovered. The recently republished book by Nan Shepherd, *The Living Mountain: A Celebration of the Cairngorm Mountains of Scotland,* promoted the previously neglected author to celebrity status, with her picture on Scottish banknotes and her book recorded in audio format.[4] In much older literature the best examples are the Icelandic sagas, which are rooted in a landscape of ice, rock and fire: the stories themselves would not make an impact without the backdrop of the unique geology and geography.

The popularity of nature writing reflects the search for connection and a bond with the environment. The challenge is for land managers and conservation agencies to encourage this by fostering new understandings beyond the older practice of simply providing a noticeboard with a few facts.

The organization Common Ground, *founded* by Susan Clifford and Angela King in 1982, recognized this dimension of 'place' and began a campaign to promote local distinctiveness as a method to engage people in their local area. One of the methods used was to promote parish maps, by which people made explicit what was important to them locally. In their book, *England in Particular*, the authors celebrate 'the commonplace, the local, the vernacular and the distinctive'.[5] The aim was to tease out what in any area was important to the people who lived there.

Modern versions of these parish maps now employ existing databases which are rich sources of information, to add local colour and bring the local area to life. An example may be a digital version of the parish map, which can pull up a description of the village in the Domesday Book; an Ordnance Survey map of the farms surrounding the village with field names; a video of a recent local festival; and perhaps audio recordings of people involved in a local industry or craft. Video and audio recordings add a third dimension to the normally two-dimensional map sheet.[6]

***

A sense of place

The Greensand Ridge is a distinctive feature, crossing Bedfordshire and neighbouring counties. The ridge has been recognised as having many important habitat and conservation sites, and also includes valued recreational parklands such as Ampthill Great Park. (Photograph above by Andy Knight and below by the author)

Making a place special: selling the brand

Throughout the UK there are many places with a special identity which is recognized by the people who live and work there. What exactly makes the area distinctive is difficult to describe in words. Unless your place is a Lake District mountain or sea cliffs in Cornwall the competition to market your patch as 'special' is daunting. Areas which do have a distinctive feel then struggle to carve out a 'brand', which can be used to draw visitors or convince local people they have interesting and attractive countryside on their doorstep.

The Greensand Country Landscape Partnership (GCLP), based in Bedfordshire, with small extensions of the distinctive sandstone topography into neighbouring counties, has attempted to distil what makes this area in the centre of lowland England different.[1] The outcome is in the form of a 'toolkit' on offer for use by local businesses in marketing. The idea is that by using elements from this toolkit, a hotel or a pub can then promote the business using the Greensand brand as an additional visitor attraction. Other areas, such as the Forest of Bowland and the Clwydian Mountains in Wales, have also created these landscape-character toolkits.

This approach borrows directly from ideas of a 'sense of place', which is described in the toolkit as: 'the emotions and experiences we associate with places. It's how places make us feel'. This goes beyond the visual, also embracing sounds and past experiences, which all contribute to making a place special. It is recognized that this emotional attachment to a locality is important in the highly competitive tourist business, and the aim is that visitors develop an affinity to a place which will hopefully boost spending and prompt return visits. Improving the local economy is the ultimate goal.

Like any toolkit the exact use of the materials provided is left to the user. What works as a marketing idea for a country house hotel, will differ from the local brewery.

In the world of urban architecture, planning and design, the word 'place' has found its way into the new compound word of 'place-making'. The implication is that 'special places' can be created or existing locations modified by design, to make a memorable space within the urban environment. The role of public art is important in these initiatives to instil a sense of character within a place. This often leads to discussion on what is appropriate or even attractive. In Central Bedfordshire Council for example, four 'place-making' groups were appointed to work with local communities and help shape sustainable development. The language of the planners reflects lofty principles, such as 'harnessing community assets' and the promotion of health and happiness.[7] This trend follows planning in North America, where there is an active push suggesting such places, both rural and urban, can be manufactured, or at least made more explicit. In Britain the question is how best can the countryside accommodate this trend? How can public engagement be harnessed to engage the public in the expectation that there are benefits both for the individual, as well as for the protection or conservation of a specific site or landscape?

This is often done through investments in countryside interpretation centres, where the elements of a landscape are explained. In northern Britain, The Sill, perched on the edge of Hadrian's Wall, combines a study centre, an education resource and a straightforward visitor attraction, which greatly enhances a visit to this spectacular slice of wild Northumberland. Local farming, sheep breeds, folk legends, history and local characters are all woven together with the fundamental geology which shapes the land. This creates a picture of a living landscape in which people earn a livelihood, as well as welcomes the many visitors. National Parks have invested heavily in telling the story of the landscape which they seek to protect. Building a narrative, with the land and its people at the centre, has become an aspiration, whereas formerly, the traditional noticeboard or interpretation panel would have been deemed adequate. Recent thinking has complemented this static approach, with innovative ideas such as outdoor theatre re-enactments, storytelling and sculpture. Meeting a troop of Roman soldiers camped on Hadrian's Wall has taken a few modern long-distance walkers by surprise!

There has been much academic interest in attempting to unravel the way in which people connect to nature and landscape. The University of Derby is leading this field in the UK and has appointed a Professor of *Human Factors and Nature Connectiveness*. Research from this group has led to the National Trust setting out pathways for engaging and connecting the visitor to their sites and areas of protected landscapes. The previous approach of simply passing on facts – for example, 'these rocks are 100 million years old' – has been replaced by communications using the senses, emotions and a quest for meaning. The idea is to build a deeper relationship with the natural world through an understanding of what makes a place distinctive.[8]

At the heart of this search for an authentic place is the recognition that local action is central. Local village plans, parish maps, the rising interest in the formation of community orchards, pocket parks and forest schools are all rooted in the understanding that people are willing to act in defence of their immediate local areas. The rise of volunteering to work with national and local organizations in maintaining parks and gardens is a practical effort to express this local involvement. The challenge is injecting these values into the national thinking and shaping this to make a wider difference.

Throughout this book runs a thread which traces how and why the countryside is likely to alter significantly in the coming decade. Although the urge to plant trees in an effort to counter climatic change is strong, this may dramatically alter an area which is central to how people feel about *their* landscape. In the same way, rewilding may offer opportunities for biodiversity and wildlife while, at the same time, limiting access to a dog walker or the use of a bridle path. Finding the balance may not always be simple. There will be competition between interest groups, including the basic notion of the countryside as a larder, with food security a priority. The depth of feeling centred on conserving a locality is often underestimated. Consultations which involve what planners call 'a change of land use' can be exhaustive, lengthy, fraught and expensive.

Change may be not be embraced by all but the essence of the British landscape has always been that new crops, and farming methods alter the land and what we see over the hedge. We live in a dynamic countryside and what we see today is a reflection of the way in which the countryside is used presently, with an imprint left by the history of past use. What we see as distinct in an area will reflect people, farming and former rural industry. The French concept of 'terroir', originally a term used in the wine industry to capture the essential character of a specific site and its impact on the grape, is now used more widely as a description of landscape. Therefore, 'place' can be an artificial landscape shaped by human effort. When widespread sheep farming was abandoned in parts of the South Downs in the 1930s, the ecological/conservationist worry was that open chalk grassland would revert to its natural scrub. Much time and expense are now expended on clearing 'encroaching scrub', to ensure the open Downland landscape associated with Thomas Hardy is what we see today.

A sense of place is now recognized as important in both a personal way and as part of national identity. The National Parks and other designated areas protected for their intrinsic beauty or scientific interest are a symbol that people care, expressed both at the local and national level. At the international level, World Heritage Sites are sources of pride and bring a responsibility to protect and cherish areas such as the Salisbury Plain Neolithic sites or the Hadrian Wall Roman landscapes.

CHAPTER TEN

What Will Work?

The intention of this book has been to unravel some of the issues which face the land and the countryside in Britain at the start of 2020 and the ensuing decade. The departure point has been that the speed of change is increasing and there are opportunities to think differently about what we expect from the landscape. The approach has been to treat each of these potentially radical changes separately, as this is the only possible way to achieve clarity and, at the same time, try not to miss the interconnections. Although agriculture faces potentially significant shifts in the level and method by which the taxpayer will provide a farm subsidy, these adjustments will take place against a background of a changing climate. Added to this are the emerging trends in what we demand as healthy food, and a growing awareness of a range of other demands now expected from the land. Sarah Bridle in her book, *Food and Climate Change without the Hot Air*, pointed out that most people will first experience climate change through the availability, choice and cost of the food they need.[1]

The big questions at the heart of this are: What is the countryside for? How is it best used? In 2017, the Royal Society of Arts (RSA) made an effort to tackle these questions, and the RSA Commission reported in 2019 and made the links from changing demands and preferences in food, to changing farming, leading in turn to a changing countryside and, beyond that, to a changing world. The global nature of the food and agricultural industry is best illustrated by one statistic from that report: for every 100 hectares farmed in the UK, 70 hectares are farmed elsewhere in the world to meet UK consumption. The final report, entitled *Our Future in the Land*, starkly sets out the dilemma.

> *Decades of policy to produce ever cheaper food have created perverse and detrimental consequences. Farm gate prices are low; and whilst food in the supermarkets is getting cheaper, the true cost of that policy is simply passed off elsewhere in society – in a degraded environment, spiralling ill-health and impoverished high streets. The UK has the third cheapest food amongst developed countries, but the highest food insecurity in Europe.[2]*

These arguments were acknowledged in the opening of this book. Food production has always been the major influence on the countryside and this is unlikely to change. The 140,000 farm businesses in the UK are in listening mode, waiting for signals on how the new subsidy and support framework will operate. Although only around one per cent of people in the UK are employed in agriculture, around 72 per cent of UK land is farmed. People are an essential part of this landscape: they both shape it and are shaped by it. Any change in the way in which a subsidy is paid will, in turn, impact on the land and how it is used. As a result, this will influence land available for tree-planting, the ability to store carbon from the atmosphere, wildlife and conservation, leisure use, flood control and, ultimately, what we see over the hedge. There are likely to be tensions among keeping cheap food on the menu, ensuring supply and meeting the other demands on the land. These will be political choices and farm businesses are understandably concerned about their future.

The idea that the countryside has many roles other than simply producing our food is now well established. The term often used is a 'multifunctional landscape'. These ideas are not new – the hedged enclosure landscape of the Midlands counties was designed with parklands and woods, in which the hunt was not encumbered, and was almost as important as the agriculture. The modern shooting estate is planned to achieve the optimum returns for a variety of enterprises, including forestry, grazing, arable land, income from holiday cottages, fishing, revenue from windfarms and shooting rights. What is now changing is the difficulty in setting priorities. How can the countryside achieve the best outcome to arrive at 'public goods' which will warrant the investment of 'public funds'?

Following the financial shock of the Covid-19 pandemic, it has become clear that substantial new money, new laws and new organizations to spearhead any transition to a new normal in the countryside are most unlikely. For agriculture – the major land-use activity in England – the new provisions within the Environmental Land Management System (ELMS) are the only initiatives on the table. Farmers will need to explore innovative ways to harness the financial benefits on offer by embracing novel ideas which, in the past, they have not seen as part of their primary role in producing food. Those with a stake in the way we farm have broadened their interests, to include urban communities interested in public access, cleaner air, animal welfare and the reduction in the flooding of their local street. At the national level the pressing Government imperative is to store carbon, mostly using increased tree cover, and restoring areas of upland peat. In England, the Government is in the process of consulting on both a national tree and peat strategy, both due in 2018.

Britain is not alone in searching for balance. Across Europe the tension shared among intensive commercial agriculture, making space for nature and combatting global warming, is also a lively public debate.

As visitors to the countryside, we bring with us perceptions of what the landscape *should* look like, influenced by the pastoral views of the National Parks and a lengthy historical period where not much has appeared to change. Ian Hislop described this in a BBC2 programme as 'a green imagined land', which was deeply felt throughout Britain, but nevertheless nostalgic and often fanciful.[5] The countryside has become a 'storehouse of national identity', now exploited by the heritage industry.

It is important to set this in context. In the immediate post-war period until the early 1970s, Britain had turned its back on the rural past and there was a much-needed drive to modernize the countryside. Rural electrification in the 1950s was backed by reforms to farm tenancies and the application of technology to the farming sector. Machinery became bigger, more expensive and more efficient.

The number of farmworkers declined and coniferous plantation forests spread over the marginal hill lands of northern England, southern Scotland and Wales.

The downsides to these countryside changes are now, in retrospect, obvious, and include the loss of farmland birds, the grubbing-up of hedges and, in many places, the uprooting of ancient woodland. Also, there was a personal cost: farm businesses became more indebted and farmers felt isolated and uncertain. There was a feeling that conservation would need to wait until times were more prosperous. The expansion of agriculture at the expense of biodiversity was seen to be in the 'national good', both as an export industry, as well as a buffer against national food insecurity. By the early 1980s the tide was turning against the wholesale landscape changes and observers such as Howard Newby realized that: 'an irreplaceable part of the cultural heritage, a living record of the past and a potentially productive contribution to the future', was disappearing.[6]

A new conservation movement began to win support, which challenged development and farm intensification at the expense of nature and won several significant battles. Effort was concentrated on nature reserves and areas of special scientific merit, and planning enquiries became hotly debated tussles over newts and rare butterflies.

An imagined countryside – parkland landscapes

A picture of parkland landscapes with characteristic features such as a grand house set in a park with mature trees, water features and grazing animals is firmly fixed in the perception of what the English countryside should look like. Often, as here, the stamp of the great English gardeners is still evident and celebrated. In many cases these parks are now part of a working agricultural environment The Shuttleworth estate is now a college teaching land-based skills. (Photography by Lisa King)

Can we learn from others? A look elsewhere

The interlocking questions of food security, land use and climate change are not unique to Britain, and it is interesting to look at how others are approaching the adjustments necessary to cope with change. In Europe, the Dutch have also grappled with the dichotomy of historically high levels of funding support for commercial and intensive agriculture, versus a low-intensity more environmentally friendly farming approach. History as elsewhere plays a part. The wartime experiences of the Netherlands during what became known as the 'hungry winter' of 1944–45, when some 20,000 people died before liberation, shaped the Dutch attitude to food and has influenced Dutch agriculture since 1950. The phrase often used is 'never again', which has dominated the attitude to food security. As in Britain following the end of rationing, food production was a priority across Europe. It is no accident that a Dutch Minister of Agriculture became the first European Commissioner for Agriculture and the architect of the Common Agricultural Policy (CAP), which set in motion the system of subsidy which ultimately resulted in overproduction and led to butter mountains and wine lakes.[3]

In the Netherlands there is now an emerging pushback against the overriding role of commercial farming on a very limited land base. On one hand is the argument that the will need to maintain a premier position as a food producer in the global market: dairy products, tomatoes, eggs, onions and potatoes are all major exports. Add to this the country's leading role as a producer of flowers and plants in Europe, and the pressure on the land is substantial. On the other hand there are rising levels of pollution and environmental unease. There has been rising support for conservation measures, including the rewilding of polder land originally destined to be farmed. The swing in popular thinking is illustrated by allowing some hard-won polder land to return to wetlands.

Leading academics in the Netherlands are already asking these questions and when the University of Wageningen publishes scholarly articles entitled, 'Is agriculture in the Netherlands running up against its limits?' then there is public concern. It is becoming increasingly difficult for farmers to combine nature conservation with intensive production. The Dutch Government has adopted innovative new policies, which have been described as 'nature-inclusive'. However, there are underlying problems in these gaining wide acceptance. The policies need to prove they are worthwhile and the public needs to embrace this idea of nature-inclusive farming.[4]

It's not so different from Britain.

The Lawton Report in 2010 examined the present status of Britain's tattered nature reserves and conservation areas, and concluded these protected areas were not in a good state: many reserves were too small to be effective; they were not linked to each other and so failed to encourage wildlife on any scale; and finally, there were simply not enough protected areas in the first place. One outcome of this is that wildlife populations have become more and more genetically isolated and lack variety, which is an inbuilt buffer during a time of environmental change. A few nature reserves would not fix the problem of a decline in wildlife and, as Newby pointed out, life outside the reserve fence would be grim overall for British wildlife.

The urgency of the rewilding, described simply as the 'wilding' movement, spearheaded by Isabella Tree at the Knepp Estate, is at the leading edge of this new thinking. In her thought-provoking book she acknowledges the change in perception this would require both by the general public, the farmers and land managers.[7] Much as the idea of beavers in the streams of the West Country is appealing on a nature programme, the thought of lynx in the Northumberland hills is anathema to a shepherd.

Driven by concerns over climate, especially amongst the young, the pressure for conservation efforts is growing. There is a consensus that the present network of designated sites and small isolated nature reserves is not working, and conservation areas and good practice needs to be part of the farming landscape. The lever to promote this is the farm subsidy, which rewards good stewardship but would need to be bold and move beyond the previous position of a few trees in the corner of a field or a wider field margin. However, the proponents of wilding may have some way to go to convince the conservative rural population that the traditional adherence of careful land-management can be suddenly thrown over.

Whatever the changes, there are likely to be battles over land: as an investment; for housing; as a strategic food-producing area; as a new forest; for renewable-energy generation; as an overspill storage area for flood water; or as a managed nature reserve. There is unease over the way in which the market in land is working and this, as always, will be intensely political, and influenced by a growing concern by younger people over climate, wildlife, health, diet and access to the countryside. Set against this are past frustrated efforts to rethink income from land ownership.

***

What is clear is that the future of the countryside will mean making choices and agreeing to trade-offs. Many of these choices will be contested and there will be those who lose out. The future of the countryside we want, or expect, may become as political as other social issues such as housing or schools. Economists have been handed the task of estimating the costs and benefits of these alternatives and providing some guidance on value. These financial arguments will never be accepted by all and placing a value on nature will remain an emotive issue.

These arguments are not new. There has been a lengthy history of public discourse across Britain, well summarized in an Howard Newby's book, *The Countryside in Question*.[8] This title is still apt for the present, some thirty years and more later. It is difficult to improve on some of the conclusions from the readable text. Newby also concentrated on the impact of farming and wrote:

> *Farms are multipurpose enterprises. The natural beauty of the countryside and the health of rural communities are interdependent. If the livelihoods of the rural people are undermined the countryside itself will become less attractive.*

One of the assumptions behind this short book is that there is a rising interest in the countryside, coupled with some degree of misunderstanding and perhaps confusion. This is related to a feeling that, as a nation, we have become so divorced from the reality of farming and food production that we can only relate to rural life through the of the landscape in a protected nature reserve. One drawback of this is that reserves can become 'honey-pot' attractions for visitors, which are ultimately detrimental to the habitat, defeating the purpose of the protection.

Although the trend to move out of the city to a village, if only as a weekend retreat, is still strong, the graft of earning a livelihood from the land is only folklore for the majority of the twenty-first-century British population. James Rebanks' book on the challenges of shepherding in the Lake District makes this point clearly.[9] A greater interest in countryside matters is beginning to take root and is fuelling a new perception that the countryside must be allowed to change, otherwise it will become a museum condemned to being both socially and economically in decline.

What is encouraging is that we have woken up belatedly to these pressures and there are rafts of ideas on how to implement the increasingly urgent changes. Suggestions range from rewilding tracts of the landscape, to an upsurge in tree-planting, and each initiative is being argued passionately, not only in the specialist journals and by organizations, but increasingly in the national media. What is now appreciated is that not everything will work in every place. There will be failures and disappointments, and a search for others to blame when funds are spent and the outcome is a disappointment. What will undoubtedly be needed is long-term thinking, coupled with a sense of vision; large amounts of funding; a willingness to accept change; and being comfortable with some level of failure.

The 2020 Covid-19 pandemic and national lockdown focused attention on how much we value the outdoors. Hour-long walks close to home became an important and fragile link to nature for those within a short distance of a park or an accessible area of countryside. Nature became for many the go-to-place when there is woe. Planning for a recovery is set against the pressing claims to concentrate on rebuilding the economy, creating jobs and mending the health structures. The fear is that, just as in time of peace after war, the environment and nature will need to wait for a better time.

CHAPTER ELEVEN

Go Faster - Go Bolder

This book was begun when wild fires were sweeping Australia in late 2019, and the threat of the global climate emergency was becoming clear, even in Europe. Parts of the UK were suffering record levels of winter flooding and summer temperatures were reaching new heights. The final draft was completed in September 2020, when the western states of the USA were struggling with forest fires and, in England, farmers were reporting yields of wheat reduced to 1980s' levels following difficult weather conditions during the growing season.

Over this six-month period the world had been turned upside down by the coronavirus pandemic. It is too early to unravel the lessons learnt from this episode for the countryside, farming or rural life in Britain. This has not prevented many commentators trying to spot merged trends and becoming forecasters. Reports have been issued and serious articles written identifying potential opportunities which might provide a hopeful horizon. There has been a consensus that, within a 'new normal', Britain needs to reset its relationship with nature, food and farming, and the health of the population.

Although not related directly to the Covid crisis, the Wildlife Trusts document, *Let Nature help: How Nature's Recovery is essential for tackling the Climate Crisis,* contained an important message, which echoes earlier chapters in this book. The essence of this report was to tease out, with examples, where nature has achieved a remarkable comeback, given a chance.[1] Furthermore, the argument is that the 'state of nature crisis' and the 'global climatic emergency' are inseparable. Throughout this book, *How to Value a Skylark*, the message that these environmental issues are interdependent has been central: floods are linked to the vegetation and habitat in the river catchment; biodiversity can be improved by planting the right trees in the right place; and the well-being of the population is related to their access to the countryside and outdoors.

As the Covid emergency deepened, the organization Wildlife and Countryside Link brought together fifty top-flight agencies, such as the National Parks, to support a radical scheme to recruit, train and employ up to 10,000 young people in a National Nature Service.[2] Modelled on US schemes, this would make an immediate impact on youth employment and inject manpower into the schemes and projects which were already planned. The organizations estimate that some 330 projects are simply waiting for adequate funds to underwrite the labour costs. These ideas first surfaced in a 2019 report by the *Food, Farming and the Countryside Commission,* and the extraordinary circumstances during 2020 re-energized this approach by appealing directly to the public.[3]

The combined challenge of creating jobs and improving the environment is also behind the Government policy outlined by George Eustice, the Secretary of State for the Environment, Food and Rural Affairs in June 2020. The Green Recovery Challenge Fund has a

£40-million pot to spend on what the minister described as 'shovel-ready projects'. This, it is hoped, will create 3,000 new jobs and one aspiration is that these initiatives will play a part in connecting people with their environment. The expectation is that this pot of funding will be open to bids from conservation organizations such as those advocating the National Nature Service. If these projects are ready to go, then this fund will provide the funds to kick-start an environmental recovery.[4]

The new normal and the countryside

Farmers and land owners reacted differently to an increased use of the countryside during early 2020. The photograph above illustrates one response which was to close an unofficial but well used path by ploughing the headland and drilling a crop, so preventing access. The argument was that litter and fly tipping were increasing as restrictions took hold across England. (Photography by the author)

All of these initiatives and many more were floated during early 2020 as a response to the disruption caused to what everyone in Britain and beyond had long regarded as 'normal'. There was an aspiration to build something better, more sustainable, with nature and a green economy at the centre of policy. From cycle ways to waste recycling, ideas which had been seen as worthy but at the margins, were now centre-stage. In July 2020, a Government report entitled *National Food Strategy*, brought the production of farming and the food industry firmly into focus. This study commissioned by the Department of Food and Rural Affairs (Defra), held a wide-ranging consultation and the author Henry Dimbleby did not try to soften the language in his final report. His conclusions were stark:

> *Decades of policy to produce ever cheaper food have created perverse and detrimental consequences. Farm gate prices are low; and whilst food in the supermarkets is getting cheaper, the true cost of that policy is simply passed off elsewhere in society – in a degraded environment, spiralling ill-health and impoverished high streets. The UK has the third cheapest food amongst developed countries, but the highest food insecurity in Europe.* [5]

As Tim Lang points out in his urgent book on Britain's food industry, the coronavirus crisis might help to re-engineer our food-supply chain, as he argues that the emptying of shelves as a result of panic-buying may help people to: '*think about where their food comes from. It's a very simple message but the crisis, defined by some empty shelves in supermarkets, is a useful one'.*[6] The fragility of the food supply and the reliance on agricultural workers from Europe have recharged much older arguments over food security, forgotten in the dizzying choice of food to which we have become accustomed. There has been a sense that this was a 'once in a lifetime opportunity' to move to more sustainable and healthy food, with more local sources of supply.[7]

The imperative of including farmers in any discussion on future food supply seems obvious. However, as farmers' organizations never tire of pointing out, there is often a gap in understanding. The danger is that farming as a livelihood is pushed to the margins of debates on tariffs, trade, labelling and nutrition. During the lockdown period, when there was an outpouring of media attention on nature and the outdoors in general, the business of farming did not figure greatly. Partly this is connected to the size and intensive nature of modern commercial agriculture. A casual countryside visitor is unlikely to have a chat with the agricultural contractor working from the air-conditioned cab of a combine harvester that costs upwards of a quarter of a million pounds, who needs to operate constantly to make the repayments on the capital invested. Despite the best efforts of television programmes such as *Countryfile*, we are generally remote from the land and food production and are simply not sure what questions to ask.

The intention of this book was to attempt to unravel the issues which would impact directly on the countryside and farming in the decade beginning 2020. The Covid-19 pandemic early that year reordered priorities which, in the aftermath of the virus, are being rapidly reassessed. Rebuilding the economy and equipping services to cope with possible future waves of infection have become paramount. The existing concerns have, however, not disappeared, although the levels of priority may be recalibrated.

Various questions remain central: How is the climatic emergency best tackled? Is this still viewed as an 'emergency' when set beside the rebuilding of the UK economy? The present intention is to press ahead with the 2021 Climate Summit (CoP26) in Glasgow in November 2021, and it will be interesting to see if the UK goal of a carbon-neutral budget by 2050 is still thought to be attainable. There is wide scientific consensus that any slippage in reducing emissions will lead to a much deeper crisis as early as 2050. The Government's intention to move away from agricultural subsidies and pay farmers for initiatives which benefit the environment, such as the planting of trees, may come under scrutiny if the economy needs a boost. There is a danger that the climate emergency, which eventually galvanized the political class into action, will no longer be viewed as a real priority. However, there are also signs that the public is ahead of Government thinking on the climate crisis. In early September 2020, a Climate Assembly convened six House of Commons Select Committees' reports on the UK's efforts to reduce carbon emissions to net zero by 2050. This was not just another government report: some 100 people from the general public were asked to listen to a range of specialists and then debate over several months the climate issue and focus on how the country can met this ambitious target within a thirty-year time horizon. Their report, *The Path to Net Zero,* accepts the need for a voluntary change in diet to less meat and dairy, plus the aspiration of a *'managed diversity of land use'.* The assembly participants really did envisage a restored landscape with more trees, peat and wetlands.[8]

As elsewhere globally, the Covid-19 pandemic emergency has shocked the UK. The options for renewing and rebuilding the economy have become intertwined with what we have come to call 'green issues.' A green recovery is the aspiration. If this is to be achieved then trade-offs and compromises will be necessary during the coming decade. Navigating the thicket of political expediency, well-funded lobby groups and commercial interests will be a national challenge, requiring astute political footwork.

Meanwhile, during this period of disruption, political life has continued with a number of proposed initiatives which have alarmed those interested in conservation and a future sustainable countryside. As part of changes to the planning regulations the Prime Minister, made the point that, *'newt-counting delays are a massive drag on the property of this country'* – a statement which is unlikely to instil confidence in the many people providing nature-friendly environments for amphibians, nor in the general public, as the newt is a protected species. [9] This undercurrent, which is pulling away from what are seen as red-tape restrictions, also emerged in the proposal by the Environment Agency to alter the water-quality targets in British rivers. Presently, using the standards adopted within the EU and applied in Britain, only 14 per cent of rivers meet the requirement to be classed as 'good'. Under a proposed 'reform' of the standards the UK would now be free to make a water-quality judgement on fewer criteria and therefore achieve a greater number of higher ratings.[10] The water, however, will remain less than perfect.

All this is set against international efforts to reduce carbon in the atmosphere as rapidly as possible. As this book has shown, many of these issues are emotive and beyond the cool rationale of economic analysis. Although attaching monetary values to nature may help and inform debate, there will be many with passionate opposing views. The discussion will be noisy and never dull.

Finally, the skylarks ... During the lockdown spring of 2020, a few hundred yards from the newly built houses, I walked on a popular footpath crossing the wheat fields to the next village. The absence of traffic on usually busy roads and under a flight path made the skylarks' song clearer and more appealing than ever, although it was still difficult to spot the birds.

A space to breathe and thrive

The Flitwick Moor wet woodland inspired American artist Jim Trolinger to paint in the 1970s. This location is also a Site of Special Scientific Interest (SSSI). One part of the site includes former peat cuttings now flooded which now provide a range of habitats. The proximity to urban areas with easy access, makes the moorland conservation area a popular and well-used area for walkers. (Art work used with permission of Jim Trolinger)

189

NOTES

Preface

1. Cocker, Mark. *Our Place: Can We Save Britain's Wildlife Before It Is Too Late?* Jonathan Cape, 2018.
2. Population declines for skylarks. RSPB, March 2020.
3. HS2 decision will destroy precious wild places. The Wildlife Trusts, 11 February 2020.
4. Kerr, Brian, 2014 & 2019 (see Further Reading).
5. Monbiot, George. People want to create a greener, happier world. But our politicians have other ideas. *The Guardian*, 22 July 2020.

Introduction

1. Australian Fires: How do we know how many animals die. BBC *News Reality Check*, 4 January 2020.
2. *Agriculture Bill* 2019–20. House of Commons Library, First Reading, January 2020.
3. News transcript, US Department of Defence, 12 February 2002, Washington.
4. Hoskins, William George. *The Making of the English Landscape*, 1955.
5. Millman, RN. *The Making of the Scottish Landscape*, Batsford, 1975.

Chapter 1

1. How Brexit could change the face of rural Britain, *Economist*, 30 August 2018.

2. *A General View of the Agriculture of the County of Bedford: With Observations on the Means of Improvement.* Thomas Stone, The Board of Agriculture and Internal Improvement, 1808.

3. How secure is our food supply? *Telegraph*, 19 August 2009; and Farmers: UK losing battle to feed itself, *Telegraph*, 22 February 2015: Spuds, veg, and digging for victory, *The Week*, 11 April 2020.

4. *Agriculture Bill 2019–20* House of Commons Library, First Reading, January 2020.

5. ELMS versus BPS. Why waiting for ELMS is not the right thing to do. *Savills Research* Article, 12 June 2019.

6. Agriculture in the European Green Deal. Alan Matthews, *CAP Reform,* 12 January 2020.

7. Farming for the Future: Policy and Progress Update. Defra, February 2020.

8. The Brave New World of Adam Macy, Graham Harvey. BBC, *Archers* blog, 11 April 2016.

9. Only 100 harvests left in UK farm soils, scientists warn. *Farmers Weekly*, October 2014.

10. UK is 40 years away from 'eradication of soil fertility', warns Gove. *Farming Online*, 22 October 2017.

11. BBC, *More or Less,* 3 June 2020.

12. Wong, James. The idea that there are only 100 harvests left is just a fantasy. *New Scientist*, May 2019.

13. Future Countryside Programme. Royal Society of Arts, 1988. https://www: therca.org/countryside.

14. Westmacott, R. and Worthington, T. *Agricultural Landscapes: A third Look (CCP)*. The Countryside Commission, 1997.

15. Tanasescu, Mihmea. Land Abandonment in Europe: The Changing Face of Conservation in the 21st Century. *The Civil Animal*, 3 February 2017 .

16. Villiers, Theresa, Secretary of State for the Environment. Speech at the Oxford Farming Conference, January 2020.

17. Trade talks and the NFU petition. BBC Radio 4, *Farming Today*, 20 June 2020.

18. Home-grown food production is the key. NFU, 7 August 2018.

19. Farmers fear life outside the EU. George Monbiot, *Guardian*, 11 January 2017.

20. Graham, Kim, Shrubsole, Guy, Wheatley, Hanna and Swade, Kate. *Reviving County Farms*. CPRE, December 2019.

Chapter 2

1. Cited in Rackham, Oliver. *The History of the Countryside, Chapter 5*, 'Woodland'. The Ely Coucher Book is a medieval

manuscript and provides a record of the Church estate, including woods, pasture, meadow, fisheries and farmland.

2. Shrubsole, Guy. General Election: Party pledges on tree-planting. Friends of the Earth, 25 November 2019.

3. Budget Statement, March 2020.

4. Harvey, Fiona. Tree-planting in England falls 71% short of government target. *Guardian*, 13 June 2020.

5. *England Tree Strategy*. Defra.

6. *UK Trees and Forest.* Parliamentary Office for Science and Technology, January 2007.
https://www.parliament.uk/globalassets/documents/post/postpn275

7. Government launches new scheme to boost tree-planting. Government UK, November 2019.

8. Shukman, David. Will planting millions of trees really save the planet? BBC News, 4 March 2020.

9. *Costing the Earth*. BBC Radio 4, 26 May 2020.

10. https://www.forestcarbon.co.uk, 19 March 2020.

11. Enabling a Natural capital approach. Government website.
https://www.gov.gov.uk/enabling-a- natural-capital approach.

12. First 'tiny forest' planted in the UK. *Ecologist*, 11 March 2020.

13. Monbiot, George. Put a price on nature? *Guardian*, 15 May 2018.

14. *Ancient Woodland and Translocation: The Trust's Position.* Woodland Trust, October 2014.

15. Welburn and Crambeck, Yorkshire. *Guardian*, Country Diary, 25 April 2020.

16. Wohlleben, Peter. *The Hidden Life of Trees: What They Feel, How They Communicate – Discoveries from a Secret World. Greystone Books, 2016.*

17. Maitland, Sara, *Gossip from the Forest*: *The Tangled Roots of our Forests and Fairytales*, Granta Books, 2012.

Chapter 3

1. Carrington, Damian. Hedgehog numbers plummet by half in the UK countryside since 2000, *Guardian*, 7 February 2018.

2. Tinkering at the hedges, *Raconteur Media*, May 2017.

3. Tree, Isabella. *Wilding: The Return of Nature to a British Farm.* Picador, 2018.

4. Niemann, Derek, *A Tale of Trees: The Battle to save Britain's Ancient Woodland*. Short Books, 2016, p.29.

5. Making space for nature, The Lawton Report, 2010.

6. *The Natural Choice: Securing the Value of Nature.* Government White Paper, June 2011.

7. Cocker, Mark, *Our Place: Can we save Britain's Wildlife before it is too late?* Jonathan Cape, 2018.

8. Michael Gove, speech at Kew Gardens, July 2019. Available at: https://www.wcl.org.uk/michael-gove-asks-if-not-now-when.asp.

9. Cocker, *Op. cit.*

10. State of Nature Reports. 2013, 2016, and 2019. Published by a consortium of British conservation organizations. Available at: https://www.rspb.org.uk/our-work/state-of-nature-report.

11. Making space for nature, *Op. cit.*

12. *State of Nature 2019: UK's wildlife loss continues unabated.* National Trust, 2019.

13. Estate owners across the UK are queueing up to introduce beavers. *Guardian*, 1 February 2020. Patrick Barkham.

14. Tree, *Op. cit.*

15. Scottish beavers causing trouble sent to Yorkshire. *Telegraph*, 31 May 2019.

16. https://www.wildennerdale.com.

17. Beaumont, Emily. Bison brought back to UK for first time in thousands of years. *Independent*, 10 July 2020.

18. Missing lynx: How rewilding Britain could restore its natural balance. *Observer*, 12 July 2020.

19. Farmers hatch plan to return area the size of Dorset to wild. Patrick Barkham. *The Guardian,* Patrick Barkham, 14 July 2020..

20. *Towards a wilder Britain*. The Wildlife Trusts, 2018.

21. Government statements, accompanying the 2019-0 Environment Bill.

22. Moss, Peter, *The Accidental Countryside: Hidden Havens for Britain's Wildlife.* Faber, 2020.

23. Macdonald, Helen. *The Hidden Wilds of the Motorway*, BBC Four, 30 June 2020.

24. Moss, *Op.cit.*

25. Knight, Sam. *Can farming make space for nature? New Yorker*, 17 February, 2020.

26. Harvey, Fiona. UK facing worst harvest since the 1980s, say NFU, *Guardian*, 17 August 2020.

Chapter 4

1. Carrington, Damian. This is the decade and we are the generation. *Guardian*. 15 February 2015.

2. Harvey, Fiona. UN climate talks end with limited progress on emission targets. *Guardian,* 15 December 2019.

3. Lynes, Mark, *The Final Warning: Six Degrees of Climate Emergency.* Fourth Estate, 2020.

4. *Reforms must prepare the UK countryside for climate change and ensure that our land supports reduced emissions.* Committee for Climate Change (CCC), November 2018.

5. *Land Use: Reducing Emissions and preparing for Climate Change.* CCC, November 2018.

6. NFU tackles the climate change challenge: Achieving net zero by 2040. NFU online, 1 January 2020.

7. Harvey, Fiona. *Op.cit.* 17 August 2020.

8. Harrabin, Roger. Climate policies will transform the UK landscape. *BBC News*, 1 November 2019.

9. *Assessing the potential of climatic change for the English landscape.* Natural England, research report, 2013.

10. Cook, Isabel. *Historic British Landscapes under severe Threat from Climate Crisis.* University of Sheffield, 27 September 2019.

11. https://www.archaeologicalresearchservices.com.

12. Parliamentary Office for Science and Technology. Post Note 363, September 2010, 1 March 2020,

13. Thompson, David. Preparing for the effects of climate on the UK natural environment. CCC blog, 2 December 2015.

Chapter 5

1. One explanation for this quote is that the river is a bit player in a much larger land dispute, and Hotspur is complaining not so much at the altering course of the Trent, but his land allocation overall.

2. Melting arctic ice triggers winter storms, study finds. *Guardian*, Weatherwatch, 25 July 2020. Report links storms to the rapid melting of Arctic ice and directly to global warming.

3. Humphreys, Rachel. Flooded Britain: A new normal? BBC Podcast, February 2020.

4. It was a feeling of terror: When will the water stop? *Guardian Weekend*, 29 August 2020.

5. *Flooding in England: National Assessment of Flood Risk.* Environment Agency, 2009.

6. Purseglove, Jeremy. *Taming the Flood: Rivers, Wetlands and the centuries-old Battle against Flooding.* William Collins, 2015.

7. State of Peatland in England inquiry launched, Commons Select Committee, 2 August 2019.

8. Monbiot, George. If we want to cut flooding, we should stop burning the moorland. *Guardian*, 11 February 2020.

9. Stratford, C. *et al. Do trees in UK-relevant river catchments influence fluvial flood peaks? A systematic review.* Centre for Ecology and Hydrology, August 2017.

10. Flooded Britain. *Costing the Earth.* BBC Radio 4, 26 May 2020.

11. *Tackling the Under-supply of Housing in England.* House of Commons Library, 8 March 2020.

12. *Increased spending on flood defences is not enough to solve flooding problems.* Institute and Faculty of Actuaries, 3 November 2016.

13. Lean, Geoffrey. *How a Yorkshire town worked with nature to stay dry. Independent*, 2 January 2016.

14. Right now, we abandon people. *Financial Times*, 10 August 2020.

15. *Salt marshes or sea walls? Preventing coastal flooding in the UK.* Grantham Institute, 5 December 2019.

16. The Lawton Report, *Op. Cit.*

17. *A Green Future: Our 25-Year Plan to Improve the Environment.* Progress Report, May 2018.

18. Monbiot, George. The UK government wants to put a price on nature – but that will destroy it. *Guardian*, 15 May 2018.

19. UK National Ecosystem Assessment, 2014.

20. Easton, Mark. The Great Myth of Urban Britain. *BBC News,* 28 June 2012.

Chapter 6

1. World Heritage Sites. UNESCO, 2020. See: https://whc.unesco.org/en/list.

2. https://www.southdowns.gov.uk.

3. Manley, John (ed). *Secrets of the High Woods*. South Downs National Park Authority, 2016.

4. Stonehenge: Neolithic monument found near to sacred site. *BBC News*, 22 June 2020.

5. Hewison, Robert. *The Heritage Industry: Britain in a Climate of Decline*. Methuen, 1987.

6. Giving up land is 'sacrilege'. *Hexham Courant*, 10 September 2020.

Chapter 7

1. Shrubsole, Guy. *Who owns England? How we lost our Land and how to take it back.* William Collins, 2019.

2. Giles, J. A. and Ingram, J. *The Anglo-Saxon Chronicle*. Project Gutenberg, 1996.

3. Southall, H., Baily, B., and Aucott, P. 1930s *land utilisation mapping: An improved evidence base for policy*? Portsmouth Research Portal, University of Portsmouth, 2007.

4. HS2 Rail Link. Woodland Trust, press release, February 2020. https://www.woodlandtrust.org.uk/protecting-trees-and-wwods/campaign-with-us/hs2-rail-link

5. Williams, A. and Martin, G.H. (eds.). *Domesday Book: A Complete Translation*. Penguin Classics, 2005.

6. Earl of Derby, House of Lords, debate, February 1872. House of Commons Library,

7. Bateman, John. *The Acre-Ocracy of England*. Forgotten Books, 2018.

8. Hayes, Nick. *The Book of Trespass: Crossing the Lines that divide us*. Bloomsbury Circus, 2020.

9. Cook, Rachel. Forgive us our trespasses: Forbidden rambles with a right-to-roam campaigner. *Observer*, 9 August 2020; and Monbiot, George. Landowners have stolen our rights. It is time to reclaim them. *Guardian*, 19 August 2020.

10. Country Land Owners and Business Association. https://www.cla.org.uk.

11. No sell-off for public forests. *BBC News,* 31 January 2013.

12. Collinson, Patrick. House prices aren't the issue, land prices are. *Guardian,* Money, 18 November 2017.

13. Farmland Index. Knight and Frank, 2019.

14. Pike, Ben. Who is *buying* Britain's largest farms, and for how much? *Farmers Weekly*, 7 July 2018; and Analysis: England farmland market by type, size, price, and area. *Farmers Weekly*, 23 October 2019.

15. Cited in Shrubsole*, Op.cit.*

16. *Elveden Estate: Our story.* Farm website, May 2020.

17. Wach, Elise.Rise of the 'megafarms': How UK agriculture is being sold off and consolidated. Coventry University, 5 October 2018.

18. Pearce, Fred. Sparing vs sharing: The great debate over how to protect nature. *Yale Environment 360*, 3 December 2018.

19. Tree, *Op.cit*.c

Chapter 8

1. *A Green Future: Our 25 Year Plan to Improve the Environment.* Progress Report, May, 2019.

2. *Re-evaluating Parks and Green Spaces: Measuring their economic and wellbeing Value to Individuals.* Fields in Trust, 2018.

3. Hardman, Isabel. *The Natural Health Service: What the Great Outdoor can do for Your Mind*. Atlantic Books, 2020; and Mitchell, Emma, *The Wild Remedy: How Nature Mends Us - A Diary*. Michael O'Mara, 2018.

4. Barkham, Patrick. Can nature really heal us? *Guardian*, 14 March 2020.

5. More than one farmer per week in the UK dies from suicide. *FarmBusiness*, 15 February 2018.

6. Monbiot, George. The UK government wants to put a price on nature – but that will destroy it. *Guardian*, 15 May 2018.

7. *Bedfordshire's Natural Environment: Its Value to all*. The Bedfordshire Local Nature Partnership, 2016.

8. White, Matthew, *et al*. Spending at least 120 minutes a week in nature is associated with good health and wellbeing. *Nature*, 13 June 2019.

9. *Space to Thrive*. Heritage Fund, January 2020.

10. Mabey, Richard. *Nature Cure*, Vintage, 2008; and *Common Ground: A Place for Nature in Britain's Future?* Hutchinson, 1980.

Chapter 9

1. *Spirit of Place* toolkit. Greensand Country Landscape Partnership.

2. Smith, Roly. *A Sense of Place: The Best of British Outdoor Writing*. Michael Joseph, 1998.

3. Evans, Estyn. *Mourne Country: Landscape and Life in South Down*. Dundalgan Press, 1989.

4. Nan Shepherd's Cairngorms. BBC Radio 4, *Open Country*, 14 June 2019.

5. Clifford, Sue, and King, Angela. *England in Particular: A Celebration of the Commonplace, the Local, the Vernacular and the Distinctive*. Saltyard Books, 2006.

6. Bodenhamer, David J., Corrigan, John, and Harris, Trevor M. (eds.). *Deep Maps and Spatial Narratives*. Indiana University Press, 2015.

7. *Breathing Spaces: Sites and Greenspace … Oases at the Heart of your Community*. Central Bedfordshire Council, 2013.

8. Richardson, Professor Miles. Pathways to a closer connection with nature, University of Derby blog, 6 December 2018.

Chapter 10

1. Bridle, Sarah. *Food and Climate Change without the Hot Air.* UIT Cambridge, 2020.

2. *Our Future in the Land.* Royal Society of Arts, Food Farming and the Countryside Commission, 2019.

3. Doshi, Vidhi, The small Dutch town that wants to shape the future of your food. *Guardian,* 5 March 2020.

4. Bos, J.F.F.P., Smit, A.L., and Shröder, J.J. Is agricultural intensification in the Netherlands running up to its limits? *Wageningen Journal of Life Sciences,* 66, 65–73. 2013.

5. Hislop, Ian. *Olden Days*, Episode 3: 'Green Imagined Land', BBC 2, 25 March 2020.

6. Newby, Howard. *The Countryside in Question*, HarperCollins, 1988.

7. Tree, *Op. cit.*

8. Newby, *Op. cit.*

9. Rebanks, James, *A Shepherd's Life: A Tale of the Lake District.* Penguin, 2016.

Chapter 11

1. *Let Nature help: How Nature's Recovery is essential for tackling the Climate Crisis.* Published by all the Wildlife Trusts in the UK, June 2020.

2. Carrington, Damien. 'National Nature Service' needed for green recovery in England, groups say. *Guardian*, 22 June 2020.

3. *Our Future in the Land, Op.cit.*

4. Ballard, Oli. £40 million green jobs challenge fund announced. *Business Leader*, 6 July 2020.

5. Dimbleby, Henry. *National Food Strategy: Part One.* July 2019.

6. Lang, Tim, *Feeding Britain: Our Food Problems and how to fix them*. Pelican, 2020.

7. Briggs, Helen. 'Once-in a lifetime', opportunity for more sustainable food. *BBC News*, 29 July 2020.

8. *The Path to Net Zero.* Report of the Climate Assembly UK, 10 September 2020.

9. Harrabin, Roger. Boris Johnston newt-counting claim questioned. *BBC News,* 3 July 2020.

10. Laville, Sandra. Diluting English river standards, a backward step, campaigners warn. *Guardian*, 21 August 2020.

Further Reading

Bridle, Sarah, *Food and Climate Change without the Hot Air*. UIT Cambridge, 2020.

Claire, John, *'The Skylark'*, from The Poetry Foundation: https://www.poetryfoundation.org.

Cocker, Mark, *Our Place: Can We Save Britain's Wildlife Before It Is Too Late?* Jonathan Cape, 2018.

Dimbleby, Henry, *National Food Strategy: Part One*, Government Report, July 2020.

Figueres, Christiana and Rivett-Carnac, Tom, *The Future we Choose*, Manilla Press, 2020.

Hayes, Nick, *The Book of Trespass: Crossing the Lines that Divide Us*, Bloomsbury. August, 2020.

Hewison, Robert, *The Heritage Industry: Britain in a climate of decline*, Methuen, 1987.

Hewitt, John, 'Landscape', from *Selected Poems*, edited by Michael Longley and Frank Ormsby, Blackstaff Press, 2007.

Hoskins, W.G., *The Making of the English Countryside*, Hodder and Stoughton, 1955.

House of Common Science and Technology Committee, *Natural Capital Accounting*, Post Note 376, May 2011.

Kerr, Brian, An *Unassuming County: The Making of the Bedfordshire Countryside*. Eventispress 2014.

Kerr, Brian, *A Certain Degree of Magnificence: People in the Bedfordshire Landscape.* Eventispress, 2019.

Lang, Tim, *Feeding Britain: Our Food Problems and How to Fix Them,* Pelican, 2020

Lawton, John, *Making Space for Nature*, Department of Agriculture and Rural Affairs (Defra), 2010.

Lyne, Mark, *The Final Warning: Six Degrees of Climate Emergency,* Fourth Estate, 2020.

Mabey, Richard, *The Common Ground*, Hutcheinson, 1980.

Mabey, Richard, *Nature Cure, Vintage*, 2008.

Maitland, Sarah, *Gossip from the Forest: The Tangled Roots of our Forests and Fairytales.* Granta, 2013.

Millman, R.N., *The Making of the Scottish Landscape*, Batsford, 1975.

Moss, Stephen*, Accidental Wildlife: Hidden Havens for Britain's Wildlife*, Faber & Faber, 2020.

Neimann, Derek, A Tale of Trees: The Battle to Save Britain's Ancient Woodland, Short Books, 2016.

Newby, Howard, *The Countryside in Question,* HarperCollins, 1988.

Pryor, Francis, *The Making of the British Landscape*, Penguin, 2010.

Pye-Smith, C and Rose, C., *Crisis and Conservation: Conflict in the British Countryside*, Penguin, 1984.

Rebanks, James, *The Shepherd's Life: A Tale of the Lake District,* Penguin, 2016.

Revels, Richard, and Bellamy, Graham, *Bedfordshire: Our changing habitats and wildlife,* Bedfordshire Natural History Society, 2020.

Shepherd, Nan, *The Living Mountain,* Aberdeen University Press, 1977.

Shrubsole, Guy, *Who Owns England? How we Lost our Land and How to Take it Back*, William Collins, 2019.

Smith, Roly, *A Sense of Place: The Best of British Outdoor Writing.* Michael Joseph, London, 1998

Tree, Isabella, *Wilding: The Return of Nature to a British Farm.* Picador, 2018.

Warwick, Hugh, *Linescapes: Remapping and Reconnecting Britain's Fragmented Wildlife.* Vintage, 2017.

Wildlife Trust, *Let Nature Help*, June 2020.

Winter, Michael and Lobley, Matt, *What is Land For?* Earthscan, 2009.

Wohlleben, Peter, *The Hidden Life of Trees: What They Feel, How They Communicate - Discoveries from a Secret World* William Collins, 2017.

INDEX

A

B

flooding, 92

    -coastal 103

fly tipping, 183.

Forestry Commission, 137

Forestry England, 42

forest schools, 153

food

    -security, 6, 10, 13, 28,

    -standards, 2,27

G

glaciation, 65

Green Recovery Challenge Fund

Greensand Country

    -Ridge, 115, 162

Greensand Country Landscape Partnership, 117, 163

Green Recovery Challenge Fund, 182

grouse moors, 16, 95

Gove, Michael, 15, 20,59

H

habitats

    -heathland, 85

Hardy, Thomas, 168

Harman, Isabella, 149

Haynes, Nick, 135

Mind charity, 149

Mitchell, Emma, 149

Moggerhanger, 46

Monbiot, George, 150, 156

Moss, Peter, 74

N

National Farmers Union, 24, 26 ,81, 82

National Food Strategy Infrastructure Commission, 130

National Nature Service, 182

National Parks, 24, 27, 166, 168

   -Exmoor, viii

   -Lake District, 64, 86, 159,163

   -South Downs, 121

Natural England, 84

National Trust, 60, 63, 124, 135, 166

natural capital accounting, 2, 44, 105

nature recovery networks, 72, 73

Neimann, Derek, 56

net environmental gain, 76

Netherlands, 38, 175

   -Utrecht, 157

New Scientist, 21,

Newby, Howard,173, 177, 179

newts, 187

NHS, 148

Brian Kerr's other publications:

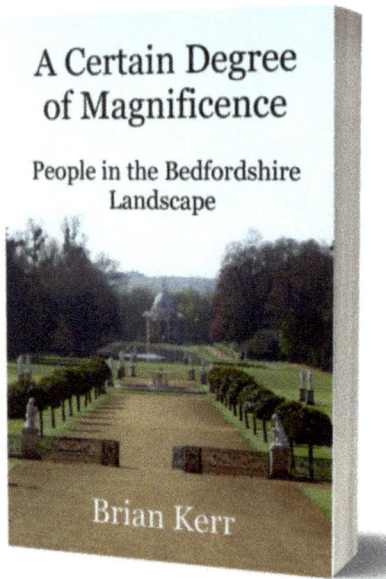

A Certain Degree of Magnificence traces the history of the Bedfordshire landscape highlighting the impact of the many individuals who have shaped the appearance of the countryside we enjoy today.

This book will appeal to those who are interested in history and the outdoors and are curious to learn more of the people who worked and lived close to the land, from the arrival of Norman landowners to the extraction industries in the 20th century.

The book is well illustrated with colour photographs and includes a useful appendix listing and describing the numerous locations mentioned in the text.

ISBN: 978-0-9932608-6-5

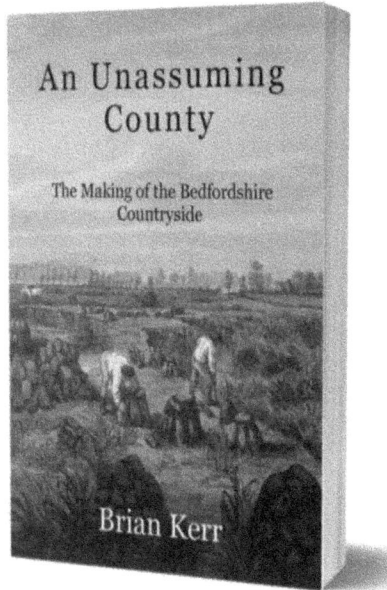

An Unassuming County sets out the foundations of the landscape in Bedfordshire and traces the way in which the fundamental geology has influenced the way in which has way the land is used today.

By focusing on one English county the author explains in non-technical language how the rocks and episodes such as a period of ice cover has moulded the shape of the modern countryside.

The illustrated text will also be of interest beyond Bedfordshire, to anyone curious about what they see on a country walk.

ISBN: 978-0-9572520-9-7